THE FERRIS WHEEL

Also by Richard Syms
Working Like the Rest of Us

Richard Syms

THE FERRIS WHEEL

Searching for an Adult Faith

SCM PRESS LTD

Copyright © Richard Syms 1988

British Library Cataloguing in Publication Data

Syms, Richard
The ferris wheel.
1. Christian life. Faith
I. Title
248.4

ISBN 0–334–00470–5

First published 1988
by SCM Press Ltd
26–30 Tottenham Road London N1 4BZ

Typeset by Gloucester Typesetting Services
and printed in Great Britain by
Richard Clay Ltd, Bungay, Suffolk

CONTENTS

An Introduction   I

1 A Sense of God   9

2 Jesus – The Shape of God   27

3 The Unleashing of God   46

4 All You Need is Love?   65

5 The Coming of the Kingdom   94

6 Together   120

7 The Word and Other Words   148

8 Glimpses of Eternity   167

9 At the End of the Day   190

   A Kind of Credo   211

   Notes   213

An Introduction

This book arises out of a perceived need. The reader may find himself or herself disagreeing with every word and every argument put forward in the chapters that follow, and yet I would still defend from sheer personal and practical experience that the exploration that they represent needs to take place. It is now almost ten years since I gave up full-time ministry in the church, and began to earn my living in a secular environment, in my case as an actor and director in theatre and television. In that time, as well as having to thrash out for myself what my ordination meant in that context, I have also met and come to love many people whom we used to call 'good pagans' – people whose hearts and minds are stretching towards the same things as my own, sharing aspirations with mine, even though mine have arisen out of specifically Christian experience and theirs have not. Indeed, the Christian faith is something that most of such people have rejected, because in their perception, it bears no relation to the issues that they actually care about. That is more than sad; it means, if only in terms of resources, that the churches are missing out on vast numbers of people who have the love, the enthusiasm, the will and the wit to change the world in the name of Christ. Somewhere along the line, we have shaped the Christian faith into a form that is unacceptable to such people.

I remain old-fashioned enough to believe that Christianity is intended to be a missionary faith. I believe that the world would be a better place if more people were fired with the Christian vision, locked into its resources, more closely in touch with the revealed source of love. The society we live in draws further and further away from love and compassion, hope and vision. It is a very special kind of society that has exalted 'trivia' to the status of a serious quest, or even a board game to be taken seriously. It is a sign of deep unease and a total lack of genuine concern that enables a national newspaper to carry a headline as trivial as 'Charles and Di in TV triumph' simply because two members of the Royal Family appear on television. We can retreat easily into such unreal fantasies, but they are frankly no longer funny. There are too many people in our country and in the world who are unhappy, desperate, hungry, homeless, suicidal, frightened, to allow human life to continue down such a road. The need for the salvation of the world is itself desperate, and to achieve it God needs those who call themselves Christians to encourage into the fellowship or at least to work alongside all who share our ideals and could articulate them to the world. To do that, such people must come to respect the faith we proclaim. Frankly, at present, they do no such thing – there are too many obstacles in the way. Most are obstacles that Christians have placed there for their own defence, their own security and comfort. If we really care about the salvation of the world, if we really care about mission, then I submit some of them will have to go.

What intelligent, grown-up people see is a variety of stunted and childish forms of Christianity. Most Christian apologetic, or at least most that ordinary people encounter, is of the 'take it or leave it' kind. It's not put as crudely as that, but that is what in effect it is – those paperbacks that purport to explain and proclaim the faith, but which in fact pre-suppose everything they are about to prove, and the pre-suppositions are ones which the world in general simply does not share, so that no grown-up is ever going to get past page one. This can come from the evangelical end of 'The Bible says . . .' or the catholic end of 'The church believes . . .' It doesn't make any difference. Either way, it is simply jargon, and if what is being said is relevant to real human beings, it is made inaccessible, not through lack of painstaking patronizing or sophisticated video techniques, but simply because massive assumptions are being made which most people just do not share. Whole debatable areas of myth and philosophy are presented as indisputable facts in a way that is too much for most people to take. This presumably gives the 'preacher' a pleasant feeling of superiority –

I can believe things that you cannot – and the satisfaction of having preached the gospel, and it is not his or her fault if people ignored it . . . It does not occur to him or her that as far as 'people' were concerned, he or she was talking or writing gibberish. Real mission, real evangelism will be far less glib, far more costly. It will have far more to do with dialogue, and will care more that minds and hearts genuinely meet.

In the United States, this autocratic, 'take it or leave it' Christianity has reached sinister depths – pseudo-conversions across the airwaves, vast sums of money being solicited and manipulated for very dubious causes, and an unholy alliance of religious fervour with extreme right-ring politics. The signs are not far away in Britain. We have hectoring right-wing politicians who seek to hi-jack the concept of morality and use it to mean a revenge pattern for order and law, an excuse for pushing sexual discussion and activity back into the closet, an insistence that the poor and disadvantaged should be silent and satisfied with their lot. Killing foreigners, making vast sums of money at the expense of others, are coming to be seen again as virtues. For the world's sake, before such distorted ideas become the norm, it is important that the facts not the fantasies of Christianity are heard. Because Christians are tacitly accepting the inverted morality of the bigots, the people who ought to be Christians or aligning themselves with us are rejecting that vicious expression of it which they see above the parapet, propounded by those whose sense of morality is in truth from the gutter. But we are allowing its stench to rub off on us.

There is, of course, an acceptable face of Christianity, which eschews such viciousness but which is so soft and naive that it is still not going to set the good pagan on fire. Even if he or she dodges the jargon of the self-satisfied evangelist or the bigotry of the hang 'em and flog 'em brigade, they will not be attracted either by the media soft-sell that daily or weekly presents Christianity as a hill-walking, van-travelling, hymn-singing soporific, making it appear that being a Christian is primarily about being superficially nice to everybody, especially nice to the disabled, talking in smooth voices and sitting in armchairs. Those who present or sell religion on radio and television often look and sound charming, but when you get to the end, and look back at the actual content of what is being offered, it is non-existent. Hours of words and pictures go by with nothing at all having been said, let alone anything that would provoke or challenge. It is such a frantic attempt to please everybody that it does no more than act as an anaesthetic against the harsh realities of the world.

All these out-front versions of Christianity are fantasies, they all dodge the real issues, and yet these are the forms of it that non-Christians see and reject. They are all childish in the sense that they recognize some Christian truths, but do not accept the real responsibilities of the faith. They are Sunday School stamps to go in the book, so that we may earn a prize, perhaps a Bible, at the end of the year. They are the result of accumulated rubbish. I long to stop having to say to people whom I respect, 'Yes, I know Christianity looks like that, but the really important things are the ones that Christians appear to ignore . . .' What follows is a personal attempt to clear away the clutter, or at least to sort out what is important and useful in the faith, and what accretions have simply become a hindrance to mission. As I say, you may disagree with the decisions I make in the process – what I keep and what I reject – but I would stand by a determination that the process must be undertaken if Christianity is not to be the domain of selfish charlatans.

I have no illusions that the enterprise is either novel or radical. Part of the continual struggle of valuing and living by religious experience is to filter and discriminate between what is real and useful and what is no more than self-indulgent. For all human beings who have not already limited their truth to a package of sterile assumptions, the quest for a living and relevant truth is as old as time itself. In the Old Testament, Isaiah has an almost unique understanding of mission – he knows that for God to be revealed and made active in his world, the barriers of the children of Israel had to be pushed out – 'Go out of the gates, go out, pre-pare a road for my people; build a highway, build it up, clear away the boulders; raise a signal to the peoples. This is the Lord's proclamation to earth's farthest bounds: Tell the daughter of Zion, Behold, your deliverance has come' (Isa. 62.10–11). I want to play my part in my own generation in going out of the gates, clearing away boulders, raising signals. I want to declare the coming of deliverance to the sons and daughters of my own time.

And very early on in the life of the early church, the boulders began to accumulate: the extras began to cling to the faith like limpets, to make those 'inside' feel safer and superior. Hence Paul writes to his young friend Timothy: 'Proclaim the message, press it home on all occasions, convenient or inconvenient, use argument, reproof and appeal, with all the patience that the work of teaching requires. For the time will come when they will not stand wholesome teaching, but will follow their own fancy and gather a crowd of teachers to tickle their ears. They will stop their ears to the truth and turn to mythology' (II Tim. 4.2–4). We are once again in the days when Christian truth is seen as mythology, when its most naive and egocentric expressions are increasingly popular because the jargon, the bigotry, the soft sell all tickle the ears.

For the sake of the good people I know, I want to stand humbly in the tradition of Paul and Timothy in looking for simple truth, because I want to share with them the conviction, the good news, that Christianity actually works, that it is a faith both living and credible, that it is a view of people and the world that can be held by sensible, grown-up people who want better things in life than hyped evangelism, Victorian values and Songs of Praise. The thing does actually make sense without cutting your brain in half. The particular vision of Jesus of Nazareth, if you discard the clutter around it, is relevant and workable, and a ministry, a service to the world arising out of that vision, is redeeming and healing. I have discovered for myself over the last decade that even an ordained ministry makes sense, and that for all the bizarre sensation of being a worker priest in the entertainment business, the ministry has even displayed itself in the most traditional ways of baptisms, marriages and funerals. The faith holds water in the right context and when presented in an intelligible, relevant way.

Let me forestall one criticism. In seeking to present my faith in such a way, I shall be accused, I know, of offering Christianity without its supernatural elements, since those are the elements with which my contemporaries have difficulty. Much of what I wish to tell them is that Christian faith is not a pious, religious activity, but a totally human and natural one. That conviction arises out of my understanding of incarnation, that the gap between sacred and secular, heaven and earth, God and humanity has been irreversibly closed, that the Christian life is by definition a secular one and not a spiritual 'trip'. To that conviction, my argument will need to return again and again. And that is, in fact, what I mean by 'super-natural'. I do not mean the antithesis of 'natural'; that would be 'unnatural', 'false', 'mythological'. The super-natural is, on the other hand, the natural, the real, the truthful, pushed to its godly extreme, to the point where we discover ultimate and absolute values and truths. I seek for a genuinely super-natural religion that arises out of and then empowers my natural existence. The 'boulders' are not the supernatural elements of the faith, they are far simpler, more childish things. What I want to find for myself, and be capable of offering to my friends, is a grown-up Christianity that incorporates neither the fictional or the downright silly. It is those elements that I wish to be honest enough to face up to and strip away.

Which will leave us, I wish, with a reasonable, credible understanding that will be a proper response to the natural quest in human beings for a true religion. That quest works at the two levels of personal and social. Personally, you, I, we seek some kind of fulfilment, a sense of happiness and well-being, consciousness of our own freedom, to be in relationship with other persons. These are natural, human needs that make us feel human, as we say. An adult faith needs to offer us those things as individuals, to deepen our knowledge of ourselves, so that we become liveable with, for ourselves and other people. The quest for religious experience is partly one for deep personal peace and satisfaction. It is also a search for a view of the world and the universe that makes for intelligible living in community and society. It needs to have implications that are social and political. It needs to give me a basis of thought from which I can play a reasoned part in the world in which I live. Over-personalization of faith leads one to ignore the real needs of community, over-socialization becomes bleating political slogans into the wind without any roots to them. An adult approach, a grown-up Christianity will seek the relationship between the two, between the personal and social gospels, and refuse to use either as an escape from the other.

The religious questions are eternal, serious and adult; they are asked by every human being of any sensitivity at all. Who am I? Why am I here? How do I fit in? What is the world meant to be? Is there any meaning? Are we going anywhere? They are adult questions, and they deserve answers that are not jargon or bigotry or soporific, not untruthful, fantasy or ill-thought out. They deserve grown-up answers.

I fancy this introduction is also a dedication. I want to frame my faith in a way that will also make sense to people I know. So I dedicate these chapters to those who have offered me love, understanding, community and vision, and I offer in gratitude, albeit inadequately, my experience of Christian faith. And what I seek to offer is a defence of that faith which will be to them attractive and convincing, but which is also true to the central convictions and commitment of Christians through the ages.

ONE

A Sense of God

We have to begin with God. We really do. As a good evangelical,
I would like to begin with sin: as a good Catholic, I would like
to begin with the church: as a good radical, I would like to begin
with love. But the twentieth-century seeker is quite right – you
cannot begin to discuss a religion of any kind and avoid the
question of God. 'Do you believe in God?' is the basic religious
survey question, to which, we are told, some eighty per cent in
Britain reply 'Yes'. The question begged in such a statistic is what
was meant by 'God' in the question, and what was meant by
'God' in the replies.

So the very first problem is, as it always was, the problem of
language. When I was training to be a clergyman, I was among
an irritating group who, whenever God was mentioned, which
in a theological college tended to be fairly often, would immediately pose the question, 'Now what exactly do you mean by
that word?' There really was no point in going on with any
further discussion if we were going to use words of which we did
not know the meaning. It must have driven others round the
bend. All productive discussion was stifled before it began. Of
course, sooner or later, we have to admit that no one knows
exactly what we mean by 'God' – in one sense, it is in the nature
of the word that we should not – and that, for practical purposes,
or at least, so that we can talk about something else sometimes,
we have to agree on some generalizations about what we mean
by God. We were foolish and counter-productive in persistently
asking the question. But that is not to say that the question does
not, or should not, exist. In future discussion, the question has not

been resolved, only recognized as counter-productive. In other words, no definition of God was ever arrived at; all that happened was that enough common ground was assumed to be able to converse. And that will always be true of talk about God; A's view of God may be quite different from B's, yet they can speak about him because they are able to assume enough to know what each other are talking about. If A and B addressed themselves to the direct question of what they meant by the word 'God', they might well be in total disagreement. What A must not do is claim that B does not believe in God, because B's definition of God does not coincide with his own. That is what is happening when we hear of bishops or theologians who (shock horror), we are told, do not believe in God. Over and over again, they and we reply that we do believe in God, but we reserve the right to have our own opinion as to what we mean by 'God'. But, bishop or theologian, you do not believe in God in any traditionally accepted sense. But what on earth does that mean? Does it really mean any more than 'You do not believe in God in the same way that I believe in God'? And if that is all it means, does it matter?

What I am saying is that there is no objective, mutually accepted, dictionary definition of 'God'. Let the rationalist plead how he will, there is no way anyone can speak of the existence of God as 'true' in the same way as the existence of this book as 'true'. There may be some people who think they can. But they are wrong.

For practical purposes, you and I know what we are talking about when we say 'God', although strictly speaking, my definition has arisen out of my experience and yours out of yours. It may be that my definition will allow me to do certain things with the idea of God that yours will not, and vice versa, and that may make hackles rise, but neither of us can deny the other the right to have his own understanding of what he means. The 'traditionally accepted' sense in which God is defined is the accumulated experience of others. You may well find that two people who have such a view of God may differ considerably if they addressed themselves directly to a definition. Or even if they could produce words that matched from some ecclesiastical jargon, they may never define those words either, so it could still be that their experiences of God are quite different. In God-talk, each person must, I believe, reserve the right to know and believe in what he or she means by God. What he must not do is to make that particular question so obsessive that we never reach those parts, those aspects of God that relate to human experience as a whole. If you have your definition of God, I have mine, and never the twain shall meet, then we are totally bogged down, and there is nothing else to say and no further to go. But that is not true to human experience. So we ride the definitions, we agree to accept that discussion about God is possible, and go on to primary question number two – does God exist? Is it just a word to be defined, or is there a God?

As I suggested, if the question is, does God exist in the same sense that this book exists, then the answer is probably simply No. It was an amazing form of naiveté that prompted the Russians to announce with pride, after their first venture into space, that Yuri Gagarin had not found God. They really believed that it proved something. It was based on the very strange assumption that twentieth-century Christians necessarily have an ancient Hebrew scientific view of he universe. Though presumably such an impression must have been given by some twentieth-century Christians! There may be some people who are able to believe (and this is a formula that I suspect we may hit again and again) that heaven is out there in space somewhere, that God lives in it, and directs operations from there, but I and many other Christians do not believe it for a second, and to 'believe in God' does not mean that you have to believe that. God is not, I am sure, 'out there' in any sense, either as an old man in the sky, a grown-up's version of Santa Claus, or as a supernatural Captain Kirk. The question of 'where' is itself a totally space-bound one, and if we mean anything at all by 'God', its meaning is of something unrestricted by time and space. It may even be that the word 'exist' is itself misleading when applied to God. I think I understand what Paul Tillich means by saying that God does not exist at all, in the sense that he is beyond existence, and that we should speak of God 'being' rather than 'existing', that we should rather say 'God *is*'.

Thus 'Is God?' Still a valid question, and still one that has been explored through the centuries. Traditionally and philosophically, all the arguments for the existence of God, the being of God, reduce to three. The principle of the first, named the ontological argument, is this; that if the Idea of God exists, then God must exist. Man would never have envisaged God if there were no God to envisage. The argument is stated in its simplest form by Anselm. If, he claims, there is such an idea as a Perfect Being – 'quo maius nihil' – there is no distinction between its essence and its existence. That is to say, if God is to be thought of as a Perfect Being, then part of his perfection must be his existence, that it would be a contradiction in terms to think of a Perfect Being as non-existent. But, in Anselm's apparently simple argument, there is a presupposition, an 'if', and he is dangerously near assuming what he sets out to prove. Descartes raised the argument again in a slightly new form: 'On close inspection I find that it is obvious that we can no more separate the existence of God from his essence than we can separate from the essence of a rectilinear triangle the fact that the sum of its three angles equals two right angles or from the idea of a mountain, the idea of a valley.' But, as Kant pointed out, this is only the linking of two ideas, the *idea* of God and the *idea* of existence. It does not prove that one follows from the other. The weakness of the argument is that it has no premise. The sceptic will rightly maintain that we have proved no more than that men have an idea of God. The fact of the idea cannot tell us anything about the validity of its content.

The second argument, the cosmological, rests on a notion of cause and dependence in answering questions about the origins of the world. 'You must begin somewhere,' it says. 'Even if you trace things back to the smallest atom, you still have to ask where it came from.' This argument has a premise all right. It begins from observed features in the world. The problem is that it proceeds from those features to something beyond the cosmos, by positing a Prime Cause who is other than and transcends the world. Here in the world, we have 'z'. We know that 'z' was caused by 'y', and that 'y' in turn was caused by 'x'. Sooner or later, we end up with 'A', which caused everything else, that is, God. What we have is a chain of cause and effect, of which God is the beginning. What the argument fails to realize is that it has only posited a first cause, a first link in the chain, it has not proved the existence of a God outside and beyond the chain. And, strictly speaking, it has not actually proved the first link; there is no reason logically why the chain of cause and effect should not stretch back to infinity. If God is not outside and beyond the causal chain, then he is part of it, and he himself is also an effect that demands a cause, and on we go, back to infinity. And still no God.

The third of the classic arguments is that from design, known as the teleological. Aquinas described it thus: 'We see things which lack knowledge, such as natural bodies, act for an end, and this is evident from their acting always, or nearly always . . . so as to obtain the best results.' In other words, all inanimate things work towards a purpose, and such a cosmos requires such an intricate ordering that it could only have been devised by an intelligent and purposing mind. Most of the arguments from the beauty and order of creation – 'see how the stars follow the same course each night' and so on – spring from this one. The basic logical objection is that it is an argument from analogy, that is to say, what it says is, 'Animals are like machines and nature is like a machine: machines have designers: therefore nature has a designer.' It is logically false – nature is not much like a machine. Aquinas has, however, met this objection to some degree with his phrase, 'so as to obtain the best results'. He does not argue for God from the *fact* of a designed world, but from its beneficent purpose, its value. As an objection, Kant's is probably again the most valid – that a watchmaker only puts the pieces together, he does not make them. The argument at best only indicates a designer, not a creator, or a God, let alone tell us anything about the nature of God. But what the contemporary mind finds most unsatisfactory about the argument from design is that it is afraid to consider the possibility of random chaos. Just as the first cause argument is unwilling to see the chain stretching back to infinity with no beginning at all, so this one ignores the possibility that over an infinite amount of time and through an infinite number of mutations and stages of evolution, something may have been produced which has within it some things that look a little as though they have been designed. The argument does not allow for chance, or at least underestimates what, given an infinite amount of time, chance could achieve. An infinite number of monkeys sitting at typewriters, battering at the keys, could, after a genuinely infinite amount of time, produce an intelligible book.

All three arguments, and it is probably fair to say that all other cases made out for God's existence are variations on one or other of them, have to the twentieth-century mind the smell of desperation. They feel like an attempt to shore up against the possibility of chance, of chaos, of anarchy, of meaninglessness. The case for God in this generation must not rest on this premise, anyway. He must not be a God of the gaps, if only because such gaps as there are in our knowledge and understanding of the world are now looking distinctly closeable. God is not to be used as a bastion against advance, either technological or philosophical. In fact, one suspects the motives of those who seek to argue logically for the existence of God in these times. Certainly, we must be free to say that there is no logical proof for his existence, there never has been, and never will be. To attempt one now would be to mis-understand the nature and meaning of God.

So – the word 'God' carries its own meaning for the one who uses it, and there is no way to argue for his objective existence. Is there anywhere to go? I have spent a little time on the classic argu-ments, because within each of them is a loop-hole – not a flaw in the objection – but a clue, I believe, to a meaning that we can sensibly give to the idea of 'God'. Let me work backwards through them. In the objection to the argument from design, the analogy of the monkeys does not actually destroy the argument, it merely points out that the design does not of necessity prove a designer. A believer in God may still maintain that a designer is a more probable explanation than random chance. The monkey analogy does not, after all, work the other way about. You may not prove from the fact that the works of Shakespeare are intelligible that they were written by a team of monkeys battering at typewriters. So the door for positing a designer of the universe is still open, *if you choose to posit it.* That is the crunch – there is room for choice, for a belief, for faith. The question then becomes not 'Does God exist or not?' but 'Why should I choose to believe that he does?' Not 'Can I logically prove his existence?' but 'Can I provide reasonable grounds for the choice that I have made?' The absence of logical proof does not force one into a totally negative position.

The question, though, must still be a valid one to ask. Take another look at the cause-and-effect argument; for each observable feature in the world, we ask the question 'why?', and we are pointed to its cause. Thus if a child asks 'Why do I exist?' the answer, the step before in the chain is, 'Because your parents made you.' That is a truthful answer, from within the chain, from within the series of cause-and-effect. But that may not be the question the child is asking. It may mean 'Why do I exist – ultimately?' It may be looking for an answer outside the series. So we cannot get to God by following the series. But the human spirit is not satisfied with a simple chain of cause and effect. Every time we ask 'why?', we are in effect asking two causal questions, one about the series, and one ultimate question about meaning outside the series. This observation does nothing at all to prove the existence of God or anything beyond the chain. But just as the argument from design leaves room for human choice of beliefs, so this argument indicates that the choice to search for meaning, the decision to believe in answers from outside the series, only arise from the questions that we are already asking.

And so, in a sense, we are back with the first argument, the ontological one. The questions are there, the idea is there, and so we seek the answers, we posit the reality. We choose to believe in God. Tillich expressed it thus: 'The question of God is possible because an awareness of God is present in the question of God. This awareness precedes the question.' No evidence, nothing proved, but something that springs out of human awareness. And an element of that awareness is, as Tillich goes on to point out, unconditional, persistent, absolute, so that the awareness 'transcends subjectivity and objectivity, that is, a point of identity that makes truth possible'. We have not, we cannot prove the existence, the being of God. But there is in human nature a sense of the divine, an awareness of Other which persists and refuses to be denied. It rears itself with every question we ask which demands an ultimate answer, and it forces us to look at an intricate creation, and say 'Maybe' rather than 'Nonsense'. Man carries within him a sense of God that has broken out in an infinite number of times and places, of individuals and communities.

But what is this 'sense of God'? Can it be justified? Do we really have grounds for going any further?

In the late sixties, Peter Berger, a sociologist, made an intriguing case for the supernatural that arose out of his view of society. In his book *A Rumour of Angels*,[1] he lists what he calls 'Signals of transcendence' – hints, events, clues, signs that lead human beings to suspect that there is an Other, a kind of focussing of those feelings that 'there must be something'. I have a feeling that in their original context, Berger tends to make these 'signals' feel like bits of evidence, and it is important, I think, that they are not seen as strictly empirical data. They are a subjective interpretation of human feelings. That does not invalidate them or render them worthless in any sense, but it would be false to raise them above the level of 'experience' to one of 'evidence'. But what the 'signals of transcendence' do open up is the possibility that many experiences that we regard as merely human in fact have connotations that are religious, ultimate.

To give a few examples of the kind of thing Berger means by 'signals' – he suggests that in human life, there is a fundamental awareness of *order*. A mother comforts her distressed child with the words 'It's all right'. Is she lying? Or is it that at moments such as this, she communicates her own rarely-articulated belief that ultimately, it is 'all right'? That the statement transcends the mother and child and implies a truth about an ordered reality? Indeed, Berger says, 'every parent takes upon himself the representation of a universe that is ultimately in order and ultimately trustworthy'. Or again, he points to the sense of timelessness, of eternity, that becomes our experience when we are aware of *play*. The intention of playing games, of 'homo ludens' is happiness, and to achieve it we enter the time-scale of the game. Thus all experiences of happiness, of joy, of exhilaration lead us to a sense of a playful universe, beyond time and space. 'All joy,' wrote Nietzsche, 'wills eternity – wills deep, deep eternity'.

Berger points out as another 'signal', our persistent willingness to *hope*. Human experience is always moving to the future; we continually give ourselves points of hope, and it is hope that draws out acts of courage and loyalty. Psychologically, morally, we almost naturally assert life, strength, survival over death and decay. 'A "no" to death is profoundly rooted in the very being of man.' Berger even makes *humour* a 'signal': 'The comic reflects the imprisonment of the human spirit in the world . . . By laughing at the imprisonment of the human spirit, humour implies that this imprisonment is not final but will be overcome.'

The 'signals of transcendence' prove nothing, but they illustrate that the awareness, the sense of God, precedes the question of God. They are delineated shapes of what mankind has always suspected, that there is Other. That he is not alone, represented in mediaeval myths by angels and devils, and in modern myths by alien spacecraft and ET. Something of which we know little, which is by definition totally other than us, and yet of which we yearn to be a part, with which we search for relationship. It is to this sense of God that the *vox pop* replies that it believes in God. The reply is, in effect, 'Well, there must be something.'

That reply, that 'sense', that awareness preceding the question does not, of course, arise from any philosophical discussions about the existence of God, or, for that matter, any sociological interpretations of everyday feelings. It is drawn for most of us far more crudely from moments of high experience, fleeting points of excitement, flashes when what we are and do seems to gel with a total understanding of life. Such moments we cannot explain, define or even always admit to, but they linger in the heart and mind, they become the points of truth by which falsehood is judged, streams of light that show the darkness up for what it is. Nothing can prove the existence of God, but belief in God is reasonable and justifiable as a way of recognizing this awareness, of coming to terms with religious experience. And it is important that we do not limit 'religious experience' to heightened experience about or in the context of religion or religious ceremony. In such a case, God is no more than a receiver of wishful thinking. No, what we have to recognize is that 'religious experience' is a natural human activity, that vast areas of normal human experience has ultimate overtones. 'Why?' is written in, the awareness precedes the question. We may stifle it, castrate it, deny it, repress it, just as we do instincts of death or sex. But like them, it will not go away. To repress it may be as dangerous as the repression of any other human instinct. The search for God, the beginning of a path to following a 'religion' is the facing up to that part of us which stretches out to the Other. To refute all belief in God as a total nonsense is to deny that that aspect of man exists. If I am to embrace all that I know of myself and my world, illuminated by what I have felt at the highest moments of my life, then I find I have to believe. Just as I have to acknowledge with honesty my mortality and my sexuality, so I have to acknowledge my search for the Other, my movement towards the beyond and above. Like Henry Miller in *Sexus* – 'I believe, I believe. I believe because not to believe is to become as lead, to lie prone and rigid, forever inert, to waste away . . .'[2]

Religious experience, in this broad, natural human sense, this 'sense of God' comes at us in various ways. Each man and woman, in a way, to his or her own. But it is probably fair to point to three main categories of experience in which the 'sense of God' is often most heightened, and the pinpointing of them gives us the first glimmer of indication as to the kind of God we are to believe in. As a first category, I would isolate *creation*. When the psalmist shouts 'The heavens declare the glory of God', he is not expressing the argument from design: when the writer of Genesis provides two accounts of the creation of man and his world, he is not putting forward a scientific explanation of anything. They are both responding in a natural human way to the glory of the created world, and that within it which leads outside it. The natural human way – coming over the brow of a hill and seeing a vast landscape poured out in front of you, the stark grandeur of mountains, the peace of the lakes, the free wind in the hair, the warmth of green grass or rolling hills, the sheer vastness of desert, the power of the sun, the stillness of moonlight. To each his own. For myself, drawn back to sunset over trees and the sound of children singing, a brown slatted inn in the Swiss mountains, the sun gleaming across the water between the islands off the west coast of Sweden. For you, many other different things. And not just nature! The intricacy of the human body – what a piece of work is man! No, not the argument from design, rather an argument from stunned wonder. That amount of intricacy, that amount of detailed development and evolution for no purpose? That is what I would call unreasonable to believe. And within the same category, I would place the creations of creation, the web created by the spider, the nest by a bird, the arts by men and women, a painting by Turner, a symphony by Mahler, a climax in a play by Ibsen. All creations of the creatures of the universe. And by some miracle, able to open up the sense of wonder, the sense of God in others. My involvement with the artist's sensations can become my own 'religious' experience. There is no wonder that from the beginning of time, the gods have been discovered in the process and in the sheer aesthetic power of a created world.

Almost as deep as man's wonder at his world is a second place where he looks for gods, a second category of his experience where he is aware at times of a sense of God. That is in *history* and events. Man at an early stage connected his awareness of the Other with the day-to-day running of his life. He sacrifices to the Other so that his crops may prosper. This is the result of his innate suspicion that the course of the world's history, and even the things that happen to him at a personal, domestic level are not quite random. The religion of the Hebrews, the growth of belief that is recounted in the Old Testament is founded almost entirely on this notion, that God is Lord of history and events. Their suspicion, like all of them, is based on high points of experience, massive moments in their history that illuminated the rest. For the Hebrews in particular, the fact that they got out of Egypt safe

and alive towered above all others. No historical situation seemed
to them more desperate. The fact that the right leader turned up
at the right time, the fact that they actually got away with it,
pulled a whole nation out of torture and slavery, the fact that the
great divide of the Red Sea seemed to virtually open up before
them – well, you may call them chance coincidences. It seemed
more reasonable to them to see the hand of the Other in their
history. And they have never failed to see history and events in
that way. Still for us, the sense of God lurks and occasionally
breaks out in what we more often think of as luck, chance, coincidence, fate, providence. What we are truly doing is acknowledging a sense of God in events.

To each his own again. My work takes me to various parts of
the country. Two or three days before I finished a job in Coventry,
my mother was taken to hospital with acute pneumonia. I returned to London on the Saturday, and was then out of work.
She died on the Sunday night. I was able to be there as I would
not have been able for three months before, and, out of work,
was able to stay with my father in the week or so that followed.
Very rarely do I stay in London to work. Some eighteen months
after my mother's death, I was, for once, working in London,
rather a dull job, but at least fairly long term. My father went
into a London hospital for a hernia operation. It went badly
wrong, he virtually died. He was not ready to die, he needed
continual support and encouragement to supplement sub-
consciously his own will to live. Miraculously, I was working ten
minutes away from the hospital. I could be there as part of the
process without putting my job in jeopardy. At almost no other
time in the last ten years would that have been possible. My father
is alive and well. I am left with a choice between some random
coincidences that 'all worked out for the best' and a sense of God
in history and events. I find the latter more credible.

The third, and arguably, the most potent category of experience
in which we are aware of a sense of God is that of *human relationship*. In Tennessee William's *A Streetcar named Desire*, when
Blanche Dubois is first held by the man whom she believes is
going to rescue her from the degrading chaos that she has made

of her life, she utters the famous, melodramatic and wonderfully theatrical line, 'Suddenly – there's God – so quickly.' But that is true to human experience. Perhaps even more than in the clouds at sunset, more than in the quirks of fate, it is when we catch a second's contact with another human soul that the awareness of God is most blatantly revealed. To be moved with gratitude to someone else, to feel and weep or rejoice with another human heart, to be open and aware to someone else caring about me, points of trust, thankfulness, dependence, shared hope or fear. Smiles, chemistry, real contact. Here above all, the sense of God. The heightened moment is, of course, the moment of love, love at its most real, instantly recognizable, a sensation for which there is no substitute, for which we need make no excuses. Standing between lovers – in the widest sense of 'those who love each other', parent and child, brother and sister, friends as well as sexual partners – is the awareness of God, so closely tied up with it that it feels as if eternity is caught in the act of love. Hence 'I could die like this' and 'If only this could last for ever . . .' As God appears inextricably involved with the creation and with history, so in human relationship at its highest and best, it is almost as if the sense of God and the power of love are indistinguishable, as if one might almost say 'God *is* love'. And it is this last category, the discovery of a sense of God at this point that might take us beyond theism.

Let me repeat, none of this argues for the existence of God. What it does is open up the awareness that makes us more human by choosing to believe.

Before waxing too lyrical and losing all touch with reality, we must pause to acknowledge that though we may sense God is in his heaven, all is not necessarily right with the world. We may not embrace the glory of the world, without also admitting the presence of suffering and evil. This is, of course, the ultimate question for the would-be religious believer, and I cannot cope with it all in a few paragraphs. In a sense, the whole Christian faith attempts to tackle the world's sufferings head on, so it is a question that must be returned to again and again. But if at this point we have acknowledged a sense of God in our experience, then already suffering and evil at least assume their proper perspective. They are real, but even at this point, appear incapable of extinguishing the greater realities that we discover at our highest moments. In other words, suffering and evil only become a *problem* because we have already caught sight of the glory. If we had not sensed the ultimate reality of good, we would not be confused by the presence of evil – we would simply submit to it. What we in fact feel is that evil is distorted good, but not the other way round. Suffering innately feels as if it ought not to be. Simply because we have also sensed peace and joy. Toothache is hell because we also know what a mouth free of pain feels like.

The distortion of God, which we call evil and suffering, arises from our knowledge of both good and its opposite. The tree from which Eve ate in the Adam and Eve fable was not the tree of evil, but the 'tree of the knowledge of good and evil'. It is the knowledge of both and its resulting schizophrenia that distorts us and drives us mad. Interesting, too, that God's fear in the fable is that if they eat, they will become god-like, with all the breadth of knowledge that sets up pain in him. For all our highest moments, good is fundamentally distorted. Our appreciation is of both the good and its reverse. Human nature can create the massive glory and optimism of a Beethoven quartet or a Donne sonnet; it can also strain through the Tchaikovsky *Pathetique* on its slow grind towards death, or it can spit out the unrelieved gloom of the Book of Job. And at its highest, as in *King Lear*, it can exhaust itself on human suffering until a line of glittering hope appears in the sky. It is man's god-like-ness, his awareness of all that, that makes him vulnerable to pain, to suffering, and ultimately to the deepest angst of what it means to be human. And to be ready to explore the sense of God, the highest moments, is the only salvation from that.

And, in passing, we must learn to ignore the obsession of many religious people with individual 'sins'. Such mistakes, single actions, are real enough, and all of us have to deal with them, but when religion has served only to make people feel guilty about them, it has done those people a cruel and unnecessary disservice.

'Sins' are in truth merely the symptoms, the passing rash that lets us know that the schizophrenia, the angst still goes on. 'Sins' are not to be dwelt on, but cleared up as soon as possible, so that mankind can get on with finding the way through the distortion of good to achieve what is good in itself.

Our awareness of distortion does, of itself, tell us something about our awareness of God. For we discover that in the process we have credited God not just with 'being', but also with value. We have almost by chance identified him with 'good' simply because we have already regarded the distortion of our 'sense of God' as 'evil', as somehow wrong. Quite early on in an awareness of God, we come to associate God with human values. What as human beings we do is take the values that mean most to us, and push them through to their ultimate logical extensions. Our appreciation of truth, and the various relative degrees of truthfulness that we encounter in human life, lead us to believe that there is something ultimately true, which we call Truth. The same is true of goodness, love, hope and the rest of the virtues. We come to understand God as Ultimate Value, which we posit not just from wishful thinking, but from our earthly experience.

Similarly, as we understand him by extension as ultimate value, we also see him as a sum total of values, as we recognize the relation of what we call 'virtues' to each other. Polytheism posits a different god for each function, monotheism carries within it a sense of totality, of completion. The sense of God arises from our experience, it also leads us to a potential future experience. With its sense of totality and completeness, it brings out in us a sense of hope, of response to the universe, because we begin to feel our own movement towards it. To believe in God is to put a certain value on to our highest experiences. Those experiences relate to our highest values, and so we latch on to the search for God because we believe that it is also the search for our own and the world's highest good, that it is the road to becoming what we most deeply wish to be, that it is ultimately the road to where we belong, the way home.

Hence the massive biblical assertion about God that he is 'over all and through all and in all' (Eph. 4.6). The God that we sensed in fact permeates everything. A decade or so back, Bishop Robinson made a distinction between pantheism, that is, the belief that God is everything, and pan*en*theism, the belief that God is *in* everything. That second belief is thoroughly biblical. There is nothing in earth or anywhere else of which God is not part and in which he is not involved. Incudling, one might add, the sufferings of the distortion. A positive response by man to his own sense of God is not just a response to his highest moments but to the whole of life. And it makes God a total original, the force of life itself, the Ground of Being – as the sixties jargon had it – the Ground of *all* Being, the Ground of *our* Being, the Origin, the – for want of a better word – Creator. We have arrived, I believe, at something so basic, so fundamental, so primal, so all-pervading, so massive that it alone is capable of meeting humanity at its moment of deepest angst, in the middle of its agonizing primal scream. A wild dissatisfaction that only comes to rest when it finally touches the glory of what it once sensed as God. Now it remains for us as, and we experience it as, the Ultimate Other, the totally Beyond, what we technically call transcendent. God by nature, by definition, remains utterly transcendent. Whatever chumminess men and women claim, the concept of God is vast, mysterious and glimpsed only through total darkness. The sense of God can never be approached with anything other than awe and fear of the highest kind. Harry Williams, a theologian who has contributed as much to our understanding of God and love as any in my lifetime, nevertheless ultimately and humbly calls his own autobiography *Some day I'll find you*. When any man or woman feels he has a comfortable religion where he or she knows exactly where things stand, he should recall St Paul at Athens proclaiming the 'Unknown God':

The God who created the world and everything in it, and who is Lord of heaven and earth, does not live in shrines made by men . . . he is himself the universal giver of life and breath and all else. He created every race of men of one stock to inhabit the whole earth's surface . . . They were to seek God, and, it might be, touch and find him (Acts 17.24–27).

How dare I, how dare you, how dare any of us hope to achieve simply that, let alone any more?

How did we get this far? That question is not one of stunned surprise, though it may have something of that in it. More importantly, the way in which we reached the position of trembling awe before an ineffable transcendent Other will also tell us something about him. Let us be clear what we have done; we have allowed men and women their own experiences, understanding and definitions of what they mean by God. We have failed, as we must, to prove his objective existence, but we have deduced from a wide variety of human experiences and values that belief in a transcendent Other is not unreasonable, indeed, if I face up to all my experiences and values, I find such a belief more credible than a doctrine of random chaos. But the key process is that of 'deduction'. In theology, there have been two apparently rival approaches; one of 'natural' theology, meaning at its simplest, that one may reach God through a natural observation and assessment of the world, and the other of 'revealed' theology, that is to say, that we only know anything of him at all because he has unilaterally chosen to reveal himself. I am not sure that the two approaches are mutually exclusive. There seems to me no doubt that God, as God, is quite capable of making deliberate revelations of himself to men. Indeed, as we proceed, I believe we must learn to see his revelations in more places and situations than we would have thought possible. He is, after all, 'over all and in all and through all'. But in order to understand such revelations, it strikes me that we must begin with an awareness of him in everything, that we need to find first the 'natural' way through our own observation and experience. Anything else, any short cut to a revealed God, is genuinely and justifiably open to a charge of unreasonableness.

What the 'natural' process does open up to us, what we do learn from having begun to search for God, is that there is some form of communication. That the unknowable God shrouded in darkness is somehow knowable. The Ground of Being is also the Ground of *our* Being. The Beyond is also the Beyond *in our midst*. The real twist in the tail is that the transcendent Other also appears to be imminent. The clue we found way back is our awareness that God is supremely to be sensed in human love, since this makes us aware of a sense of God that can only be described as personal, rooted in relationship. There is no reason why up to this point I should not have referred to the Other as 'It'. Yet instinctively one is pulled to the personal pronoun. Part of the human experience is not simply to want to seek for God, but that we are actively loved and accepted by the universe, that whatever is there at the centre, in all and through all, is not coldly impersonal, origin, creator, designer, but carries within itself the seeds of love – warmth, compassion, concern – that not only are we seeking truth in the cosmos, but that the cosmos is reaching out to us, longing to accept us and finally surround us with love. The rest of the Christian story is to do with that final definition of God. All the other aspects of him are reached by all the great religions of the world. Honest appraisal of human experience, its glories and distortions, turns us toward the Other. The Christian experience is to seek out the personal in the divine, to create relationship, to find love at the heart of things, to utter as a result of our sensing God the unlikely and amazing word – 'Father' 'Our Father.'

Paul at Athens went on to say: '. . . though indeed he is not far from each one of us, for in him we live and move, in him we exist' (Acts 17.27). The transcendent Other is earthed.

TWO

Jesus — The Shape of God

Almost all of the great religions of the world will posit a transcendent invisible God. The majority of them believe that God is in some way accessible to man, in however fragmentary a fashion. The uniquely Christian claim – the first point at which we begin to diverge from the others – is that God was made accessible in the life and death of a particular human being, Jesus bar-Joseph, a Jewish teacher who lived in the Nazareth and Galilee region of Israel about two thousand years ago. It is a very detailed and specific claim, and once we have got beyond the question of God, it will be on this claim that Christianity must be judged. To the man Jesus, we have chosen to attribute the title 'Christos' – 'the anointed one' – and from that the Christian faith derives its name and its essence. If Christianity is not about this man, it is not about anything. The claim is that 'no one has ever seen God, but . . . he has made him known' (John 1.18).

What we have sensed of God already should mean that the principle at least should be no great surprise. God displaying himself in the created world, in events of history and in human relationship, means that it was always most likely that a definitive shape for God, a final and crystal clear expression of what he is like, would be found in the world, as an event within history and in the life of a human being in relationship with other human beings. We have also noted the awareness of God as somehow 'personal'; it is a logical step for God to be seen as a person. We have sensed God above all in the moments of human love – it is likely that we shall see him most clearly at such a moment, and in a life committed to human love. For the claim rests in the man and his life, not just on what we are taught by him. It is not simply that we are taught everything we know of God by this man, but that he *is* everything we know of God. That the concept of God, ethereal, drifting among the galaxies, 'there must be something', was given total, accurate final concrete expression in one historical figure. The man Jesus was, we claim, the actual shape of God. Not only does God create man to be like himself, man is, in point of fact, exactly like him. If we can believe such a massive claim with integrity, this will make Christianity a unique religion in that it will be a totally earth-bound faith. It will not be a speculation about other worlds and other lives, it will be primarily about man in this life in his world. It will not be a faith for dreamers or wishful thinkers, but one that is above all practical and totally materialistic. If one human being was the shape and definition of God, then humanity is the prime concern of every believer in such a God. There would be no escape to fantasy, only a religion for men and women about men and women.

So, to begin at the beginning, this man Jesus – are we sure that he existed at all? Was there such a Jew? The answer, I think, cutting through a lot of tangled thought, is probably Yes. There are not a lot of references to him outside the Gospels, but there are just a few, notably in Josephus. And there are certainly a fair number to the early Christians, people who claimed to have known him or worked with him. The references are honestly sufficient to have little doubt that the man existed. Efforts to prove that he was a community and not a person, or a drug-induced hallucination, or a fictional figure created around a cause, have frankly appeared very flimsy, and stretch credibility to a desperate degree.

Granted then, there was such a man, are we to believe what we are told about him? As I say, it has to be confessed that the vast bulk of material is found in the New Testament, and particularly in the four Gospels. And we cannot fail to admit that all that comes from within the early Christian community, and so is unlikely to be unbiased. Thus we must to some extent face the question, 'How trustworthy are these accounts? Do they tell us anything about this Jesus that is worth believing?' The truth is, of course, that the Gospels themselves are something of a hotchpotch and arise from a variety of people, times and places. It is unlikely that the thing was recorded in any formal sense until some thirty years after Jesus's death, and some scholars would put some parts of one Gospel well into the second century. Part of the problem was that Jesus led people to expect that he was coming back any minute, and so they quite simply saw no need to keep any records. So the material we have comes at us from a variety of sources. Some bits appear to have been handed down by some kind of oral tradition, and these are usually recognized as being the stories or sayings that crop up in more than one Gospel. In other words, it is assumed that different writers drew on the same oral tradition, and that this pre-dates the written records, thus bringing us slightly nearer to Jesus's own time. Also the Gospels themselves were written down in Greek, and sections look as if Greek was the original language, that is to say, they were written by people who spoke Greek, and not spoken in Aramaic by teachers or fishermen. But there are other sections that, by their structure particularly, translate back into Aramaic very easily, and these sections are often regarded as the nearest we get to the authentic historical Jesus. The 'Abba Father', the Lord's Prayer, is a striking example of this, and it is very likely that it was spoken by Jesus himself. The Gospels as such are a conglomeration of material, at different stages of authenticity, from accurate quotation from Jesus himself through, at the other extreme, to words put into his mouth by perhaps a second-century Christian who never knew him, but wished to make a theological point of his own. Obviously scholars differ very widely as to which is which, and how late or early specific bits and pieces were spoken or written, and that is only to be expected. But to go the other extreme, and assume that the four Gospels are a simple historical account of what happened between AD 0 and AD 32 (and there are some Christians who will assume so) is frankly just plain silly.

If nothing else, we have to admit that the people who wrote the Gospels down had axes to grind. The one credited to Mark is usually reckoned to be the earliest, as it is the shortest and simplest (though why that makes it the earliest is not totally clear – it is just as easy to abbreviate a document as to add to it!) It is the closest to a direct telling of the story of Jesus's known life, beginning with his baptism and ending with the women running away from the tomb in fear. The writer is especially interested in Jesus's death and the reasons for it, and remarkably devotes more than half his narrative to the last week of his life. He also wrestles with the question of why Jesus did not make his purpose plainer at the time, and there are thus continual references to Jesus's desire for secrecy – among the disciples who had realized who he was, and among those whom he had healed. Matthew's Gospel is the most Jewish of the four. The writer bends over backwards to show Jesus as the promised Messiah, totally within the Jewish tradition. Again and again, he points out the fulfilling of Old Testament prophecy. The story is specifically told to convince Jews that they can accept the messianic claims without betraying the faith of their fathers. In direct contrast, Luke's Gospel is about and for the Gentiles. The Jesus he depicts is almost obsessed with reaching beyond Israel, and it springs very much from that wing of the early church, under the influence of Paul which saw mission as a primary activity.

The fourth account, that attributed to John, has caused more discussion than the other three. It differs from them considerably, in style, in narrative facts (the date of the Last Supper, for example), and in theology. It has virtually no material in common with them, though the others have much in common with one another. The oral tradition appears not to have reached it. It must either have been written at the same time as the others, but from quite different sources, or have appeared much later in a quite different context. We may never know. It has undeniable Jewish elements, and yet most of its ideas and thought-forms appear designed to appeal the more philosophical Greek frame of mind. It has certainly compelled the generations with its vivid imagery and profound reflections.

These are all problems for the scholars to solve, if they ever do. For our purposes, the Gospels remain collections of stories and sayings, assembled by different people with different intentions.

Does this make them true or false? Do they provide us with anything like reliable evidence as to what the man Jesus said or did?
The answer is that they are not reliable. They are patchy, sometimes incoherent, almost always biased. They come from men or
communities already obsessed with Jesus. But neither are they
false. We can sort out fact from embellishment to some extent.
Not a word of them is like writing about Jesus now – they come
from a culture and a milieu that would understand him. I would
submit that we may not possess accurate historical accounts, but
that we have something more than a novel or an artists impression. Where we do not have the words of Jesus, we have the
words that the first believers said about him. And that is not far
away. It may be, yes, that we have to admit that we know very
little indeed about the historical Jesus, but we do have a body of
material of a sufficiently early date from people who came under
his influence that it may not matter. The twentieth-century
English dramatist Howard Brenton wrote a play, which was a
version of Brecht's play in German on *The Life of Galileo*. That
play tells us something about Brenton, and also something about
Brecht. But historical research was done, and so it also tells us
something about Galileo which has not been falsified in the process. The play's vision of him may not be deadly accurate, but it
can still be true. We have enough on Jesus to work on.

To answer the question, then, of what is known of the activities of Jesus of Nazareth, one should read the Gospels, but sensibly
and with an open mind. We are not asked to believe the un-
believable. If a story seems incredible to the point of nonsense,
and there are some that do, then we must have the courage to
ask *why* the story has been included, and regard it not as history,
but as imagery; not as a fact, but as a parable. But, by and large,
to understand Jesus, read the Gospel accounts. For this, there is
no substitute. But allow me to do just a little sign-posting, a little
stating of the obvious, a certain pulling together and interpreting
of some of the strands to see to what degree the Gospel accounts
reflect or justify the claim that Christianity makes for the
man.

We know next to nothing about his childhood, his early life, his time as a carpenter. This is hardly surprising since nobody much was around to report it; and since nobody knew who he was anyway, they would not have bothered even if they had been. In short, there are no serious accounts until, obviously, his first appearance in public. This was when he stepped down into the river Jordan, and identified himself with the movement surrounding the fanatical John the Baptist. And this is precisely the point where Mark's Gospel begins. The Jews knew about baptism – it was what you did to Gentiles when they were converted to the Jewish faith. John was propounding his absurd notion that Jews needed baptism, too. Indeed, it was not merely absurd, it was positively insulting. And Jesus's first public recorded action is to align himself with John's view. From that point begins the period of public activity which the Gospels record. It appears to be a free-wheeling, unstructured period. Where he and his friends got money, we have no idea. Perhaps he had saved it in advance, perhaps he relied on giving by well-wishers.

The first major element of his work appears to be the gathering and training of a circle of friends, disciples such as other teachers would have, as John had before him. A motley bunch of fishermen, tax collectors and others, clearly attracted first by a charismatic personality, not clearly knowing why they followed him. The sort of intimate matters that he discussed with them, the reliance on them, the commissioning of them for the future, implies that the presence of this core community was one of his main purposes. He also undoubtedly earned a reputation as a teacher in a broad and public sense; on many occasions we see him preaching to vast crowds or in public debate with religious leaders and seekers. Third, he would, like other teachers of his day, also be known as a healer, and the accounts are full of the lame walking, the blind seeing, devils screaming out of people. From the beginning, it was believed that if Jesus touched you, pain was brought to rest, agony calmed into peace. A gatherer of disciples, a teacher, a healer and, in addition, a very practical builder of relationships. He sees it as some kind of duty to mix with and involve the outcast, to the disgust of his contemporaries.

He seems almost obsessed with dining at the wrong houses and forgiving the unforgiveable.

What sort of man is he that the Gospels reveal? He is a man of immensely broad views. He is a man who refuses to condition others, or to be conditioned by them. He imposes no burdens, he is thoroughly permissive in that he allows others simply to be. He is thus a man of compassion. It comes as no surprise to learn that 'Jesus wept', or that he gave Peter a look of love that dissolved the latter to tears, or that he turns to a crowd tiresomely following him and feels sorry for them. But he is also a fiery figure – you do not call the equivalent of a bench of bishops 'vipers', 'hypocrites' and 'whitewashed sepulchres' to their faces without being so. Thus the smashing of the traders' tables in the temple is equally in character. The film world has sated itself with accounts of the life of Jesus, almost all succumbing to the temptation of making him a figure of sickly sentimentality. Ignore them, return to the Gospels. Pasolini's film *The Gospel according to Matthew* is outstanding in that its final impression of the character of Jesus is stark, angry, uncompromising, verbose, to a degree cold, certainly a man capable of raising the hopes of some and the tempers of others. And interestingly enough, that is the one film made with a script drawn totally from a Gospel account.

In an almost filmic way, the opening scenes of Mark's Gospel give us, in rapid succession, the main thrusts of what Jesus was about, the effects of his presence, and thus the traits of his character. After Jesus's baptism, before collecting his first disciples, he goes 'into Galilee proclaiming . . . "The time has come: the kingdom of God is upon you" ' (Mark 1.14–15). This leads almost directly into the first incident that Mark records, a confrontation between Jesus and a mentally ill stranger who screams at him 'I know who you are – the Holy One of God'. At a word from Jesus, the man is thrown into violent convulsions, something shrieks out of him and leaves him. Thus, at the very start, Mark has drawn Jesus as a violent and *disturbing* presence, leaving behind him a dumbfounded crowd.

In direct contrast, Mark takes us to the bedside of Peter's mother-in-law, where he presents us with Jesus as a *healing* presence. She has a fever; 'Jesus came forward, took her by the hand, and helped her to her feet. The fever left her . . .' (Mark 1.31). And then, as the sun goes down, the whole town of Caperneum is gathered at the door and 'he healed many who suffered from various diseases and drove out many devils' (Mark 1.34). When, the next morning, he healed a leper, Mark describes him as stretching out his hand to him 'in warm indignation'. Days later, but recorded directly after by Mark, Jesus heals a paralysed man with the words 'My son, your sins are forgiven' (Mark 2.5). This, of course, sets up something else altogether. This is not just disturbing or an act of healing, this is a *blasphemous* presence. 'Why does the fellow talk like that? This is blasphemy. Who but God alone can forgive sins?' (2.7). The man takes upon himself an authority that belongs to God alone – 'the Son of Man has the right . . . to forgive' (2.10). And, note well, this astounding claim, this element of his character, is shown by Mark at the very start of his account. We have hardly turned a page.

One more twist that Mark presents us with before he even begins his story. There is Matthew, collecting taxes, being sneered at and spat on, suddenly finding himself collected by Jesus. And, before we know it, Jesus is 'at table in his house' with, as the New English Bible coyly translates it, 'many bad characters'. When challenged on his behaviour, Jesus replies (laughing, I wonder, with a drink in his hand?), 'It is not the healthy who need a doctor, but the sick' (2.17). Jesus's presence is not only disturbing and blasphemous, but in terms of social respectability, downright *anarchic*.

Somewhere in the middle of all that, Mark introduces us quietly to one other feature of his personality. 'Very early . . . he got up and went out. He went away to a lonely spot and remained there in prayer' (1.35). Jesus stands also within the tradition of the solitary contemplator, the mystic. As such, he was a figure whom his Jewish contemporaries would understand. He sets himself the task of understanding and defining the aware-ness of God. And somewhere deep within him, he builds up a relationship with the Other as person which is quite unprece-dented. We see next to nothing in the accounts of the wrestling of mind and personality that went on in those hours alone, but we do see its results – in the disturbing, blasphemous, anarchic, yet strangely healing habit that Jesus has of addressing God, and speaking of God as 'Father'. I had never really noticed before, but at literally no point in the Old Testament is God referred to as 'Father'. He is compared to a father, described as like a father, but never addressed and treated as such. What Jesus is presented as discovering is a new relationship of intimacy between man and God, a relationship of son to father, which is not only unique, but shocking to the point of unbearable and anarchic blasphemy. And it must remain so to us, if we are to understand not only why Jesus offended so many people, but also the nature of his teaching.

The Gospel accounts remains our best source of information about the character and personality of Jesus. They are also the source of what we know of his teaching. What was he actually saying? Again, there is really no substitute for reading it, even if it is embellished often with commentary from the early church. But let us try to catch the main areas that he deals with, the main obsessions of his mind. He teaches in three ways. He draws lessons from incidents (as we noticed, he taught man's ability to forgive at the time of a healing); he utters pithy, proverbial sayings that would stick in the mind and be easily recalled – a common enough tradition for those who heard them: the so-called sermon on the mount (Matt. 5–7) is presumably a collection of such sayings; and thirdly, he has a remarkable line in story-telling, many of them comedies, the point of which you may or may not understand. That his stories were vivid, captivating and full of insight, as well as great fun, is borne out by the fact that children still take delight in telling and acting them, or transferring them to a modern context.

Whatever the method of teaching, one cannot help but notice that the same themes, the same priorities, come out over and over again. Jesus is concerned, for example, from first to last, to teach that Old Testament prophecy is being fulfilled in his time. When invited to speak at his home town at Nazareth, he reads from the prophet Isaiah about the prisoners being set free, dramatically closes the book and announces, 'Today this scripture is fulfilled.' It does not go down well. Again and again, Jesus points out that what is happening is the fulfilment of prophecy. Moreover, Jesus very often deliberately makes prophecy fulfil itself. This is not chance or amazing coincidence. The man Jesus actually sets out to make things happen, culminating in his quite deliberately riding into Jerusalem on a donkey. It would be nonsense to suppose that Jesus did not know that Zechariah had foretold that the Messiah would do just that. Jesus knew exactly what he was doing, and what vibrations he would set up. And that will apply at other times of apparent fulfilment of prophecy. Jesus is teaching not only that prophecies come true, but that they can be made to come true, if man cares to do so.

A second recurring theme is the presence of the kingdom of God. In proverbial saying form, it is an announcement frequently repeated – the kingdom of God, the realm of influence by the Other, is not elsewhere, but here, earthbound and wordly. In terms of time, it has arrived, it has begun, it is among us, present, imminent – the days of wishing and hoping are over. And many of the stories begin 'The kingdom ... is like this ...', each describing the kingdom, as being of infinite value, of being divisive, as being built on love and forgiveness, as being secure into eternity. The presence of the kingdom arises for Jesus, presumably, out of that new relationship that he has created with God, that breaking down of the barrier between God and himself that he seems to have achieved. It opens up the possibility of men and women as channels of the Other, as creators of the kingdom, just as they may be fulfillers of prophecy. Thus much of his teaching implicitly rejects the religion of his contemporaries where the distance is fixed between man and God, where the dark clouds around the transcendent remain impenetrable. In the stories of Jesus, a publican may say 'God be merciful to me, a sinner' and thus the disciples may join Jesus in his new-found insight into God. They may say 'Our Father'.

Just as the breaking of that fundamental barrier means the end of 'religion' in a sense, it also crashes through social and moral codes. The vast majority of the stories thus illustrate another central subject of his teaching – love for and acceptance of the outsider, the reject. The people who come to the wedding, the prodigal son, the good Samaritan, the lost sheep – again and again, pride of place, acceptance, love are offered to the people who for reasons for class, race, religion, past sins, professions, are rejected by the respectable. The stories are full of people who believe themselves secure and in favour with God who find themselves ultimately rejected because they have failed to recognize the Other in their suffering and rejected brothers. 'Anything you did for one of my brothers here you did for me' (Matt. 25.40). Such love and acceptance will often demand the ability to forgive, and it is by this route that the blasphemous power comes into man's hands. Forgiveness is also at the root of Jesus's teaching. It comes up in various forms: 'If you forgive others ... your heavenly Father will also forgive you.' It was a new moral dimension, which by extension even becomes 'Love your enemy.' That, when first heard, must have appeared to turn morality on its head. 'Pray for those who treat you spitefully' (Luke 6.28).

A last example of a recurring theme, or at least an idea which Jesus goes to great pains to impress on his close disciples. The necessary cost of following a way where the God/man barrier is broken, where religion is finished, where morality is overturned and love and forgiveness are supreme. It makes you vulnerable. It lets in a level of suffering which we did not know existed. But it is part of the package – the Son of Man *must* suffer (God forbid, says Peter); you will be hauled up before the authorities. If you think this will make you popular, you have another think coming. And 'if anyone wishes to be a follower of mine ... day after day he must take up his cross' (Luke 9.23). I am not sure that even the closest disciples really believed that until they saw it happen to him.

There seems little or no doubt that the man Jesus finally set himself on a collision course with the authorities that would inevitably lead to his death. In many ways, it would have been easier for them if he had just shut up and gone away, but it frankly appears that he was determined to provoke them. Thus there come the events of the last week of his life, recorded in great detail by the Gospels. Shunted about from the Jewish religious leaders to Herod and his court, and finally tried before Pontius Pilate the Roman governor, Jesus seems to have said very little in the way of his defence. Under pressure from the religious authorities, and in fear of an insurrection, Pilate agreed to his execution. The charge upon which he was arrested and for which he was punished was a simple, but crucial one – blasphemy. 'We have a law; and by that law he ought to die, because he has claimed to be Son of God' (John 19.7). The charge was blasphemy, of identifying man with God, of threatening the whole theological and religious structure. It was a charge that Jesus never denied.

Jesus died the lingering and vile death of crucifixion along with other criminals and dissidents. Many of his disciples scattered in despair that all their hopes had come to nothing; it was indeed one of them who had given the vital information that led to his arrest. We will never know what their hopes had been. Some had looked for the end of the world, some for political freedom from the yoke of Rome, some for more years of his love and affection. And now the man was dead, and the dream was over. If the kingdom of heaven had arrived, it appeared to have been over-run.

And from that point on, the stories become wildly confused. The Gospels begin to diverge sharply. There are stories of Jesus being seen walking through locked doors, women running terrified from his tomb, other stories of angels sitting in the sepulchre, of graves opening in Jerusalem, of a stranger walking with two disciples into the country. But from all the hysterical chaos of the accounts, two features survive in common to them all. First, it does appear that the body of Jesus was missing from the tomb two days after his death. The tomb was empty. And second, although the versions differ wildly, there were very definite claims that Jesus of Nazareth was seen walking and talking after his death.

I have to confess I don't know. Such evidence as there is leads one to suspect that something happened very much like what the disciples claimed. There is a strand in the New Testament which is not too sure, a strand which speaks of Jesus as 'exalted' by God as the Old Testament figures like Moses and Elijah had been, rather than 'risen from the dead'. But certainly three days after their total dejection, the disciples themselves were utterly convinced that in some sense the man was alive. It may be that the resurrection was something that happened to them rather than to Jesus. I think I am still powerfully affected by the argument that something of enormous proportions took place to change a totally depressed and collapsed group of men and women into a force that was to turn the world upside down, to found a movement which was to survive for two thousand years. No, of course I cannot say for sure that the man Jesus physically rose from the dead, but nor can I find any other convincing explanation for what happened.

The period in which the resurrection stories evolved and in which the belief that Jesus had come back from the dead took hold, the period in which the 'exaltation' belief was met with a story about Jesus also having been seen ascending into heaven – that period coincides with the period when the disciples were looking back over the life of the man they had known and making their assessment. Rather in the same way as we looked at the world around us, observed certain values in it, and found belief in God to be to some extent reasonable, so these men and women looked at the life and teaching and activity of Jesus and began to put certain values on it. Since the resurrection idea was evolving at the same time, it is hard to know whether it was a fact or a value-judgment. But as they looked at the life and the death, resurrection began to seem not only plausible, but inevitable. What they had seen was a human being totally committed to the forces of life and love. He had been conditioned and restrained by nothing, and there was no reason to suppose that death would restrain him either. What they had seen was a man who had developed a unique and intimate relationship with God, a collapsing of the notions of God and man into one – he even used the terms 'Son of God' and 'Son of man' as if they were the same thing. He had in fact been God, he had as a man taken on himself the authority of God and opened it up for all men. This was all that God could be. God has become man, man is free, and man has risen from the dead. It is, of course, all of a piece. This is the deliberate fulfilling of the Old Testament, this is the coming of the kingdom of God and the final breakdown of the God/man barrier. This is the ultimate instance of love and compassion, this is the Other approaching man with love, by becoming him, by identifying with him. This was always what the man was on about. In hindsight, now, of course, we understand. We are the children of God, we are his brothers, God has become us, the man was God. Of course he is alive, of course he rose from the dead.

That, I believe, was the kind of process by which the resurrection idea was clinched and the beliefs about who Jesus was grew up. They complement each other. Whatever happened two days after his death set those beliefs in motion, and the beliefs inferred from his life and teaching themselves support the inevitability of his resurrection.

And the cost? That, of course, they came to understand, was the death by crucifixion. He had, you see, been rightly executed – he was guilty as charged of the blasphemy, of believing himself to be son of God. And as son of God, as the transcendent Other, he takes on not only the prejudices of his religious contemporaries, but the full force of distorted good in the universe. If man requires to be punished for the evil of the world, this man takes it on his shoulders. You need a life? God surrenders this one. Sydney Carter states this understanding of the cross compellingly in his 'Friday morning': 'It's God that I accuse . . . It's God they ought to crucify instead of you and me, I said to the carpenter hanging on the tree.' And Jesus screams, 'My God, why have you abandoned me?' God abandoned by God, the principle of the universe split from itself, the love that is the ground of being, the beyond in our midst, becomes man, breaks its heart in the service of man. Matthew's Gospel has the veil in the temple rip from top to bottom as no man could have done it at the point of Jesus's death. The veil separated the people from the Holy of Holies which only the priest could enter once a year to receive forgiveness for the people. Now, says Matthew, in a powerful symbol, the way is open, the Holy of Holies is utterly accessible, forgiving and being forgiven is a free human process. Jesus the ultimate

High Priest has offered himself as the ultimate sacrificial victim, and as a bleeding lamb or a scapegoat has taken off the evil of the universe, has healed the sickness, set the prisoners free, forgiven mankind everything for ever.

And, at the end of the day, the haunting image of a man bleeding to death on a cross is a vision of the Other, of God, that I do not believe man could ever have wanted, envisaged or created. It is a scandal and a folly. It makes no sense at all as a definition of God. And for that reason, I believe it to be an authentic one.

Such was the value-judgment on Jesus of Nazareth that the first Christians decided to take on. As ever, they could prove nothing. But it became their experience that Jesus was alive. A new life-style, a new peace and fellowship became possible as a result of the necessary redefinitions of the notions of God and man. Ask man what God is like, and the answer was now Jesus. Ask God what man should be, and the answer was now Jesus. Hence their giving him of other names – 'Christos' and 'Emmanuel' – 'God with us'. And the word they gave to what had happened was 'incarnation' – God had become human flesh, he was totally earthed, Jesus had been the literal physical shape of God.

They also asked themselves how this had happened, by what means this incarnation had taken place. The writers of the first three Gospels seem to imply that it all happened at that first moment of baptism. In their versions, the sky opens and a voice proclaims, 'You are my son, my beloved, on you my favour rests.' They seem to believe that God took the man on at that moment and shaped the next few years. The writer of the fourth Gospel refuses to pin it down to a specific moment. If Jesus was God at any point, he seems to argue, then he was always God: 'with God at the beginning, and through him all things came to be' (John 1.2–3). He was always 'the real light which enlightens every man' (1.9). Paul's theory seems to be that Jesus only became more than a man at the time of his death and resurrection. 'In obedience (he) accepted even death – death on a cross. *Therefore* (my italics) God raised him to the heights . . .' (Phil. 2.8). 'On the human level, he was born of David's stock, but on the level of the spirit . . . he was declared Son of God by a mighty act in that he rose from the dead' (Rom. 1.4).

There was never any doubt, and there never has been within the Christian community that the incarnation happened, that God became man, though it must be said that some sections have not taken its full implications seriously. The discussion was simply about mechanics. One other theory of mechanics arose which needs to be mentioned, because it is one that, for reasons best known to itself, the Christian community took on board in a big way. I refer to the idea that the incarnation was achieved by Jesus having had a virgin birth, that Mary was his mother, but that he had no natural father. This is an odd idea to have caught hold, and there are several basic objections to it. First, it is a totally unnecessary idea – we simply do not need it to prove anything about Jesus. All the grounds for our value-judgment of him come from his life, his teaching, his death, and the experience of him as risen.

Secondly, and surprising as it may seem, there is virtually no evidence for such a suggestion, biblical or otherwise. The quotation from Isaiah 7 which is read at Christmas as a supposed prophecy of a virgin birth is nothing of the sort; it refers to a pregnant young woman, that is all. When it comes to the New Testament, the lack of evidence screams out at you. If there had been a virgin birth or anything like it, the writers of the New Testament would have known about it and used it in argument to some degree. In fact, Mark clearly knows nothing about it at all, nor does John. John indeed refers quite specifically to Jesus as 'son of Joseph – we know his mother and father' (John 6.42). Paul has never heard of it – he refers, as we have seen, to Jesus as 'born of human stock' – nor has Peter, nor James, nor the writer to the Hebrews. In fact, the idea is only mentioned in two places – the opening of Matthew's Gospel, and the opening of Luke's. Those accounts vary so wildly that it is honestly difficult to credit them, particularly as there would have been no reason to report the birth. Jesus was, after all, born in obscurity, not in the glare of publicity. Nor does it take very much to see that Luke's account naturally begins with John the Baptist in chapter 3, a

parallel to the opening of Mark's, and that the first two chapters
were added later. The genealogy of Matthew at the opening of
his Gospel goes to great pains to point out that Jesus, as the
natural son of Joseph, was descended from David, and so quali-
fied as Messiah (an opening justification to his Jewish readers),
and the natural progression is then to the opening of chapter three
and John the Baptist again. 1.18–2.23 is fairly obviously an inser-
tion, albeit a totally different one from Luke's. Which leaves us
with no biblical evidence at all. I am afraid those insertions were
put in by Christians who wanted a virgin birth story like other
religions had, or whose faith was so weak that they did not believe
the incarnation could be managed without one.

Thirdly, and most important, it is theologically doubtful. Of
course, God would be perfectly capable of arranging a virgin
birth if he wanted one. But that is not the point. If Jesus had no
human father, if the sperm that created him was impregnated by
the Almighty, then he is only half-human. He has, to put it
mildly, a head start. He bears no resemblance to me, does not
know or understand my human condition, cannot be followed
by me as my example, and cannot meet my need. In other words,
far from making the incarnation possible, the virgin birth idea
actually denies incarnation. The Christian doctrine of incarnation
says that God became man, the idea of a virgin birth implies that
God pretended, came dressed up as man, like the Greek gods
coming to earth to seduce human women.

The churches have, frankly, been less than honest on this
question. To theologians, and to any who have thought the
issue out, the theory of a virgin birth has not been taken seriously
for a very long time. And yet people who have literally known
better have served it up as if it were historical fact. Now that
it is, of course, becoming too obviously a nonsense for people
to keep quiet any longer, the man and woman in the pew are
more distressed than they need have been, since they have been
deceived for so long, and now feel more than ever that their
faith is being destroyed. Just as there will always be people who
think that God is an old man with a beard who sits on a throne
in the sky, so there will always be those, I suppose, who will

believe that Jesus had a virgin birth. But they must be taught, and understand quite unequivocally, that their belief is based on no evidence, and that such a belief is not, absolutely not, a condition of being a Christian. Indeed, those of us who have rejected the idea, and prefer to share the New Testament view of the mechanics of incarnation, probably have a stronger commitment to the incarnation itself. To lose the virgin birth theory does not destroy faith, it enhances it.

And, in passing, the virgin birth should not be lumped together with the resurrection of Jesus. They are not parallel in any sense. There is evidence for the latter and not for the former.

The value-judgment made on the life and death of Jesus of Nazareth, son of Joseph, was that he was God, that the love of the universe had been displayed in him and had come to rest in him. Once the resurrection, in whatever sense it happened, had been realized, the Jesus of history became the Christ of faith. In the Fourth Gospel, it is after the resurrection experience that the writer has Mary turn to Jesus in the garden and say 'Rabbuni' – a title reserved for God – and that he has Thomas refuse Jesus's offer of physical evidence but instead to say, 'My Lord and my God' (John 20.14–18; 26–29). It is after the resurrection experience that Jesus of Nazareth is regarded as worthy of worship as divinity. The sense in which Christians worship Jesus Christ is not as a dead hero, but as a living presence, as someone who has been experienced, sensed by the awareness of faith rather than by historical evidence. The relationship between the Jesus of history and the Christ of faith will tangle men and women in knots until the end of time. But for Christians, once again the awareness preceded the question. As with the first Christians, it becomes a matter not of what you do or do not believe, but of what value you choose to put upon what his life and person represents. Once you have placed upon it a value so high that you can only say that what he represents is God, then you have committed yourself so far that there is no going back, and he can never represent anything less. The Jesus of history passes into the Christ of faith. The evidence of his life and death can only be looked at through the eyes of belief, which is of course where the New Testament writers stand. Once you have said the man was God because you felt him to be, then God is man, and you can never look at God the same way again, or at man the same way again. They have both been totally re-defined, which is exactly what the man Jesus intended to do. What he may not have intended, but which the Christian church has done, is to re-define them in terms of him. They have made Jesus the shape of God.

Key moments in the New Testament reflected that value-judgment. It is worth more than a passing look at John 1 – 'we saw his glory, such glory as befits the Father's only Son' – or at the opening of John's first letter – 'We have seen it with our own eyes ... and felt it with our own hands ... Life was made visible.' But perhaps it is Paul that expresses it with the greatest clarity and power. He describes Jesus as 'the image of the invisible God ... the first to return from the dead ... For in him the complete being of God, by God's own choice, came to dwell. Through him God chose to reconcile the whole universe to himself, making peace through the shedding of his blood upon the cross ...' (Col. 1.15; 18–20). 'Therefore God ... bestowed on him the name above all names, that at the name of Jesus every knee should bow – in heaven, on earth and in the depths – and every tongue confess "Jesus Christ is Lord" to the glory of God the Father' (Phil. 2.9–11).

THREE

The Unleashing of God

There is something natural, almost instinctive, about mankind's search for God. The awareness, the sense of him precedes the question. God will therefore be revealed and known, in his world, in history and in the lives and loves of humanity. We will discover him not in the study but in life itself. The total revelation, the ultimate discovery that God is in fact man, was made known by Jesus of Nazareth, whose life and teaching thus demands a total re-thinking of what we mean by God, and what we mean by man. Jesus let out the God in man. There is no such being as a godless person – he is 'the light that enlightens every man' (John 1.9).

One problem remains and another problem arises. The one that remains is about the nature of awareness. In place of any empirical proof, we have posited man as a creature of sensation, awareness, emotions, and argued that much religious thought and experience can be validated because of what he senses to be true. But there needs to be a part of religious belief that validates the awareness for itself, that believes that God is more than just what men and women long for. We have to say something within the scheme of faith about communication between God and man, about how, by what channel, the sense of God, the value-judgments about Jesus are made known. If the awareness precedes the question, where does the awareness begin? Who told you about awareness? Who made you feel anything?

The problem that arises is to do with the degree to which this God has limited himself. If, as Paul said, 'in him the complete being of God ... came to dwell', then we have a God of very limited power and capacity. God has, in a sense, abdicated. In this sense, he is dead. For he has abdicated in favour of man. It releases more in man than man ever believed possible, but presumably at the same time it brings God to human limitations. At one time, those of us who held such a high doctrine of incarnation were accused of reducing God to our level. In fact, what the New Testament does is the reverse, it raises man to God's level, it makes us 'sons of God' and 'heirs . . . of the kingdom' (Rom. 8.17). But if there is any reduction of God, it is 'by God's own choice'. He has chosen to limit himself to a degree where he ceases to be godlike. This is part of the problem of the world's suffering. The incarnation means, I believe, that God is limited to a point where he may not, in fact, be able to prevent it. It means that he has dealt with suffering and death even more drastically and ultimately more effectively by taking it on himself. He never was a God on the sidelines who omnipotently allowed suffering to happen. He was a God who took on the suffering, entered it, experienced it. It is the limiting of his omnipotence to a point of total identification with the sufferer. And this remains both the scandal and the glory of the Christian faith. But what we are left with is a God who looks not much like a god, more 'a man of sorrows and acquainted with grief'. There is a part of us that must learn to understand that this is what God is, and always was. We must learn not to evade life by turning our eyes to the glowing eyes of an omnipotent heavenly deity. We must learn to follow him rather into identification with his world. But we still need God. Limited though he made himself so that we might be his sons, we still need a part of him, an aspect of him that is free enough of humanity to challenge, provoke, inspire humanity to become what God intends.

Both of these problems illustrate the need for us to experience God at yet another level, or series of levels. We need to see more faces of him. We need not just to speculate and discover divinity in the world, we need more than the holding of an opinion as to who Jesus was. We need an aspect of God that will communicate, that will be the instinct and awareness that drive us to him, and that will also hold the vision of him in our minds. We need a channel for our religious experience, which comes from him and not from ourselves. We need the ground of our being to make itself known, we need the beyond not only to have entered our midst, but to be evidenced there. We need an aspect of him which touches the blood and the pulse rather than the intellect, more than a philosophy by which we live, more of a sensation that is our life.

To approach the same gap briefly by a historical route; once upon a time, for the Old Testament, there was a God of battles, of fertility, of the prophets, a God of history and events, manifesting himself in specific times and places. Once upon a time, for the Gospels, there was a man, born, lived, murdered, seen alive, but in a particular place, with people, at specific times. Then all of a sudden, the truth dawns. The man may not be dead, we sense him alive, but he cannot be said to be there any more. The disciples are faced with nothing except their beliefs, their memories and their value-judgments. Is the Christian faith genuinely made up of those things? Or is there another face, other faces of God, that touch life itself? Are we now left to wait the outcome of creation and incarnation or is there activity? Is there a working aspect of God?

Two stories in the New Testament recount the coming of the Holy Spirit. They are quite different accounts involving different people at different times in different places; they have virtually nothing in common. That does not matter, it simply means that it is very likely that neither of them has much basis in history. What they do is present the way in which the first Christians discovered that missing face of God. They had experienced God, as we have, in creation and in history; they believed that they had seen, heard, touched him in the man Jesus. But this, too, was part of their experience of him, and increasingly became so. One account is in John's Gospel, and takes place on the evening of the resurrection:

Jesus came and stood among them. 'Peace be with you!' he said, and then showed them his hands and his side. So when the disciples saw the Lord, they were filled with joy. Jesus repeated,

'Peace be with you!', and then said, 'As the Father sent me, so I send you.' He then breathed on them, saying, 'Receive the Holy Spirit! If you forgive any man's sins, they stand forgiven; if you pronounce them unforgiven, unforgiven they remain' (John 20.19–23).

It is a private, almost intimate moment, and the Spirit appears to pass like breath from Jesus himself to closest friends. It is the Spirit of Jesus.

The other account, though more well known, has no better grounds for historicity. It is simply Luke's account of the same phenomenon. He places it six weeks after the resurrection, in public, in Jerusalem, on the feast that the Jews call Pentecost:

> They were all together in one place, when suddenly there came from the sky a noise like that of a strong driving wind, which filled the whole house where they were sitting. And there appeared to them tongues like flames of fire, dispersed among them and resting on each one. And they were all filled with the Holy Spirit and began to talk in other tongues, as the Spirit gave them power of utterance (Acts 2.1–4).

Here the symbols used to describe the experience are the more violent, primal ones of wind and fire. Here the Spirit comes upon them with such a force that it is irresistible, it whips up the disciples and the crowd into a frenzy, and foreigners in the city hear the disciples speaking in their native tongues. Peter launches into a first great apologia for new-found faith when his friends are accused of being drunk. The Christian community is born, and the account ends with the claim that three thousand people became converts as a result of the experience.

In both cases the details are perhaps unimportant. What it felt like, looked like – breath, peace, wind, fire – is probably more than words or images can describe. What the stories let into the Christian experience is an ongoing activity of God, a breaking of him out of his self-imposed limitations, an unleashing of him, so that the concept of God, the sense of a living Jesus can become continually renewable. What the early church conceived, having recognized God in a man suffering and dying, was a spiritual dimension to their experiencing without resorting back to supernatural God. What the Spirit as an idea offered to them was a continual disturbing presence that was not imposed upon them from on high, but which had been imparted as a gift to mankind. The faith was not to be based on 'Once upon a time . . .', but on an endless renewing of mankind from within.

Thus this third face of God became for them a seal, a guarantee that their sense of God as love, and their value-judgment of Jesus were right. The Spirit acted as a vindication of what they had chosen to believe. The evidence for their claims was to be expressed in the ongoing activity of God in this guise. It was the evidence of the new status of man. 'All who are moved by the Spirit of God are sons of God . . . a Spirit that makes us sons, enabling us to cry "Abba! Father!" In that cry, the Spirit of God joins with our spirit in testifying that we are God's children' (Rom. 8.14ff.). 'To prove that you are sons, God has sent into our hearts the Spirit of his Son' (Gal. 4.6). It was also the evidence of the relationship that each believer found in his new relationship with the Christ of faith. 'Here is the proof that we dwell in him and he dwells in us: he has imparted his Spirit to us' (I John 4.13). And it is the evidence that there will be a Christian future. It is the first gift symbolic of all that man will now experience now that the barrier with God is down. 'You . . . received the seal of the promised Holy Spirit; and that Spirit is the pledge that we shall enter upon our heritage, when God has redeemed what is his own, to his praise and glory' (Eph. 1.13–14). The Spirit as pledge and guarantee, as evidence and vindication because it is the definition of man's awareness of God, the part of God that is a channel by which man senses God, yet carrying within it the hope of man. Just as God becomes man, so the Spirit of God is the Spirit of Jesus which is the Spirit of man. It is the spur and driving force of man's highest aspirations. Do not denigrate them. 'Do not grieve the Holy Spirit of God, for that Spirit is the seal with which you were marked for the day of our final liberation' (Eph. 4.30).

Which is why as the early Christians explored this further

experience of God which they called the Spirit, they saw him as enabling them to achieve those qualities, those ideals which mankind inherently longs for. For example, the Spirit quickly became seen as a discerner of *truth*. It was the part of God revealed in such blazing integrity that falsehood was shown up beside it for what it was. In John's Gospel, Pilate asks Jesus 'What is truth?' – man's yearning for knowing what is true. The Spirit is the aspect of God that meets such a question, and it is no coincidence that it is in the same Gospel that the idea of the Spirit of truth is examined in most detail. The writer puts into the mouth of Jesus a long discourse to his disciples before his death, much of which is a comfort given to men about to be bereaved. And the comfort is that although Jesus is about to leave them, he will be replaced by one whom Jesus calls the 'Paracletos'. This is a word that has proved almost impossible to translate; it would probably be most sensible to leave it transliterated as 'Paraclete'. But it is a key word from the early church about what they meant by the Spirit, so we do need to stop over it.

Literally, the word means one 'called to one's side', hence the translation favoured by the modern paraphrasers is 'helper', and hence to some extent the familiar King James version 'Comforter'. Both words miss the legal sense of the word, caught in the more reputable modern translations in the word 'advocate', giving the flavour of the Spirit as a counsel for defence for man. This fits better with the writer's concern for the Spirit as a spirit of truth, since an advocate is called to sift the evidence and arrive at the truth. What all these translations miss is a teaching, didactic element, hinted at in the Revised Standard Version's 'Counsellor'. For the Paraclete stands not only as counsel for the defence, but as counsel for the prosecution, if necessary accusing in the process of establishing the truth. Where man seeks the light of truth, the Spirit is the aspect of God that crisply illuminates, whether to man's glory or to his shame. His teaching is a continual reminder in the conscience of man of the eternal values sensed in our vision of God and inherent in the teaching of Jesus. It is God actively teaching and reminding. 'The Holy Spirit ... will teach you everything, and will call to mind all that I have told you' (John

14.26). 'He will guide you into all the truth . . . he will make known to you the things that are coming. He will glorify me, for everything he makes known to you, he will draw from what is mine' (16.13–14). Specifically, the Spirit reveals the truth about the distortion of man by showing the true significance of the fact that men cannot accept Jesus as God (16.9); he reveals the truth about goodness, about the greatest human values, by showing the significance of Jesus's obedience and death (16.10); and he reveals the ultimate truth about God and life by helping man sense the enormity of the victory by man that the resurrection represents. In other words, the Spirit of truth turns academic facts, opinions and beliefs into a knowledge grounded in the truth of experience. He is in fact the witness to the truth that Jesus proclaimed. What Jesus claimed for himself, the Spirit of truth validates for us. 'He will bear witness to me . . . And you also are my witnesses' (15.26–27). The teaching of the Spirit is the ultimate truth because it is rooted in the wide-ranging experiential truth that can only be achieved by God – 'for the Spirit explores everything, even the depths of God's own nature' (I Cor. 2.10). The spirit of God is the truth about God that is revealed when we sense him. And in such a context, there is a merging of experience and intellect. It is the whole truth that the Spirit represents, and so by any truthful channel, the Spirit takes the things of Christ and interprets them to each age and each believer. The intelligent Christian will refuse to look for ultimate truth anywhere other than the active Spirit of God. This becomes an important issue when we come across slight diversions from this norm in apparently different brands of Christianity. Some will look to the Bible for authoritative truth. In fact, the Bible is interpreted anew to each succeeding generation by the Spirit. Of itself it has no life, it is impossible to bind truth to the written word. Others seek for truth in the traditional utterances of the church, whereas those traditions are no more than formulated responses to the experience of the spirit to other people at other times. Of themselves, they have no life. Truth will not be bound to liturgy or dogma either. To the Bible and the churches we must of course return, but when we do, it must be on the clear understanding that the authority is the spirit, and he may reveal his truth in any way he chooses.

Man seeks truth in a world of lies, and the Spirit is truth. In the same way, man seeks life in a world apparently committed to and dominated by death. And the Spirit meets man as the Spirit of *life*. It is the source of life, and the only purveyor of it. 'The Spirit alone gives life' (John 6.63). This Spirit is, as Paul says, after all 'the Spirit of him who raised Jesus from the dead' (Rom. 8.11), and 'will also give new life to your mortal bodies through his indwelling spirit' (8.11).

The Spirit of truth is the Spirit of life is also the Spirit of *peace*. Like truth and life, peace is a symbol of man's ultimate seeking. All the great religions strive for it – in karma, in the divine light, in shalom – that point at which restlessness stops, and peace overtakes us. It is no coincidence that in the Fourth Gospel account of the coming of the Spirit, Jesus emphasises 'Peace be with you'. The Spirit is the bringer of peace, the peace that comes from experiencing the truth and committing oneself to the side of life. And that calm within the human psyche expresses itself as surely as night follows day, in peace between people. The Spirit has a function of binding together the people of peace into a unity. Thus 'spare no effort to make fast with bonds of peace the unity which the spirit gives' (Eph. 4.3). What man stretches towards is a unifying factor that will relate him to his world and to his fellow-creatures, that will prevent him struggling in isolation. The Spirit meets him in that striving – 'indeed we are all brought into one body . . . in the one Spirit' (I Cor. 12.13).

And along with truth, life and peace, the Spirit meets man in his search for *freedom*. 'Where the Spirit of the Lord is, there is liberty' (II Cor. 3.17). 'The Spirit you have received is not a spirit of slavery leading you back into a life of fear' (Rom. 8.15). Freedom from the distortion, from the roles – Jew, Gentile, slave, free – that we impose upon each other, free above all from the pattern of rule-making and law-giving by which people try to establish authority over each other. As the Spirit of God is free, so it respects the free spirit of mankind. There is no escaping the New Testament perspective, however much we wish to qualify it, that the Spirit and the law are fundamentally opposed to each other, and it is precisely that freedom from self-imposed mores and regulations that man seeks. The freedom arises from the new status of mankind in the Christian framework of thought. 'To prove that you are sons, God has sent into our hearts the Spirit of his son' (Gal. 4.6), and it is that premise that sets up the distinction for Paul between those who live by law and those who live by the Spirit. It is a safe alternative since 'if you are guided by the Spirit, you will not fulfil the desires of your lower nature' (Gal. 5.16), but make no mistake, 'if you are led by the Spirit, you are not under law' (5.18). In practice, if, as we claim, 'the Spirit is the source of our life, let the Spirit also direct our course' (5.25), and not a pattern of law.

Such concepts – truth, life, peace, freedom – do not of themselves define what we mean by the Spirit of God. But they illustrate that the New Testament, by which we mean the first Christians, saw the activity of the Holy Spirit not in terms of religious or doctrinal belief, but in terms of human value and experience. The way in which the Spirit is constantly referred to in the context of human aspiration make it almost appear that it has been defined specifically in order to meet them. You seek for truth – here is the Paraclete: you seek for life – here is the Spirit who raised Jesus, and so on into all the human aspirations you care to mention. And they are the yearnings of humanity, not simply the wishes of the pious and religious. Indeed the Spirit as we have found it may well be more at home outside such concerns. What we are dealing with is the spirit in man that will enable him to be what he and the God-who-is-man wish him to be. Much is made within theology about the functioning of the spirit within the specifically Christian community. We will, of course, find its manifestations there, but as a by-product. The prime understanding of the spirit by the first believers, those who defined it, was as the Spirit of God, poured out, as prophesied, 'Upon all mankind' (Joel 2.28). 'I will', Peter quotes God as saying, 'pour out upon everyone a portion of my spirit' (Acts 2.17). When Paul spoke of the spirit binding us into one body, it is because 'that one Holy Spirit was poured out for all of us to drink' (I Cor. 12.13). Whatever else we understand by the experience of the Holy Spirit, it is not an experience intended for the religious elite, but for the world. It is not a religious experience, but a human one. The Christian faith does not, with the introduction of the Spirit, become a spiritualized affair, it remains a human expression of human aspiration.

What it does do is feed man (with all his striving and distortion) with the *power* that we sensed in God and saw in Jesus. Where God is too transcendent, and Jesus too past, the Spirit is there with the power of both, and making such power available to mankind. In the Lucan account leading up to the Pentecost story in the Acts of the Apostles, it is power that is promised. Jesus speaks to the disciples, 'I am sending you my Father's promised gift; so stay here in this city until you are armed with the power from above' (Luke 24.49). 'You will receive power when the Holy Spirit comes upon you; and you will bear witness for me' (Acts 1.8). The power, as is self-evident, is designed to em-power, to make things possible that would not otherwise be so, in this case to bear witness for Jesus. This was the source of Jesus's own abilities and gifts; Peter later describes Jesus as a man 'anointed with the Holy Spirit and with power' (Acts 10.38). The Spirit is the validation of the sense of God and the claims of Jesus. It is called so because it meets mankind's highest values and aspirations, and it meets them because it is the line that taps the power of creation, thus empowering, enabling man to meet them for himself. As God becomes man, man takes on the status and responsibility of a son and heir of God, and also the power that goes with it. Man has godlike power, and that is a gift that springs from God having become man, and it is also in the gift of God to impart that power to him. It is that imparting that Christians mean by the activity of the Holy Spirit.

Some Christians, and a very large number among the first believers, long to see evidence of the power in quite specific instances. Their longing is rewarded in the instances of what Paul calls the 'gifts' of the Spirit, instances of specific people or specific communities displaying specific powers. This was clearly a common phenomenon in the early church, and an increasingly common one in this century in the experience of that movement within the church that is known as 'charismatic'. There is absolutely no denying the authenticity of the experience for some people. Paul himself lists what one assumes to be some of the gifts in the twelfth chapter of I Corinthians. As examples he cites, and in this order, the power of wise speech and the ability 'to put the deepest knowledge into words': faith (interesting that the ability to believe is itself a gift, a power of the Spirit, with its implicit suggestion that there will be many without that gift still acceptable to God): the power to heal and perform miraculous events: the power of prophecy (which I assume to mean more than simply fortune-telling); the ability to 'distinguish true spirits from false': the gift of ecstatic utterance (by which we assume he means 'speaking in tongues') and last, the talent of interpreting and translating such utterances. There is no doubt that Jesus himself displayed remarkable powers, and that he promised no less to his followers. There is no doubt that such powers were indeed displayed in the early church, and there is no reason to doubt that they may be displayed again. I heard what I believe to be the authentic voice of the charismatic movement when I had occasion to interview Graham Pulkingham, who was for many years parish priest of a run-down part of Huston, Texas. He explained how he had tried every community experiment that man could devise, he had mustered all the love and social concern that he could, to deal with the inescapable fact that, as he put it, 'the lame and the halt and the blind were coming to my door, and going away in the same state as they came'. And he discovered that he had the gift of healing. I believe I heard the same authentic voice in a girl who told me it was like a spring wound up inside her that snapped and set her free to a new experience, a new level of the sense of God.

But, by the same token, I frankly suspect and mistrust those who seem unable to sell the 'conversion' experience any more and now sell 'baptism of the Spirit' instead. I suspect and mistrust those who seem to be jumping on a bandwagon, seeking to divide Christians up into classes, the charismatics and the others. I suspect those for whom the speaking in tongues, a long way down Paul's list, has become a dominant gift. Those who call themselves 'charismatics', if they wish to be taken seriously by modern people, need to remember that the gifts of the Spirit are a very broad collection of things, and that love, which Paul also describes as such, is far and away the most important, and also that the Spirit belongs to mankind and his world, and not simply the community of believers, let alone an elite clique within it. The truth is that we all have gifts of the Spirit – that is in the nature of it. There is no such thing as an ungifted person.

Take, for example, the gift of healing. A trained doctor has been given the gift of healing by God. The Christian who goes for the same result by the laying on of hands is not more gifted or less gifted than the doctor. I knew one elderly lady in a wheel-chair who did not believe she would walk again. A group of friends began to celebrate communion in her house once a month; there was no healing service, no charismatics. After a couple of years, she took some hesitant steps, she went out to social events. For the last few years of her life, she came alive again. That was not done by a doctor or a faith-healer, just a few friends. It was still a miracle, still a display of the gifts of the Spirit.

What is called 'the charismatic movement' in the contemporary church is a valid and exciting expression of the Spirit of God. But it is also a dangerously limited vision of the activity of the Spirit. It seeks too often to present confines within which the Spirit must be expected to work. It becomes too easily a self-indulgent spiritual picnic, an excuse to do nothing provided the experiences are good, a meaningless ritual of arm-raising and singing. Whereas in fact, the truly charismatic will be those who least attempt to confine. The Holy Spirit is the exact reverse of the power of God in specific people for specific purposes. It is the unleashed power of God available to all mankind.

There is a very funny moment in one of the 'Till death us do part' films where Alf Garnett is explaining to his son-in-law that God is everywhere. The son-in-law establishes that God is in the pub where they are drinking, and in that particular bar. 'Is he', he goes on, 'in my glass?' 'Well, yes' replies Alf, 'he's everywhere.' At which point the son-in-law turns his glass upside down, slams it down on the table and shouts 'Got him!' That is precisely what man yearns to be able to do with the concept of God – the Holy Spirit is the face of him that will never allow him to do so.

What Luke describes in his Pentecost story, along with the rushing wind and the flames from heaven, is a scene of total pandemonium. It is the totally uncontrolled free and powerful Spirit of Jesus, it is God let loose. It is in direct contrast to the vision of a creator ordering the universe, and of God limiting himself to the boundaries of man. No wonder the disciples were thought to be drunk. And the truth is that mankind is still afraid of such an anarchic spirit. If the face of God as a man dying was unacceptable, this is even more so. We remain afraid to let him loose, we prefer to keep God where we choose to put him, we do not like God moving away from where we wish him to be. We cry for freedom, but when faced with the free Spirit of God that can make us free, we retreat to a sense of law and order. We yearn for power, but when real power is unleashed on us, we fear its getting out of hand.

The Holy Spirit is a view of God that makes it all too late for such fears. 'The spirit that God gave us is no craven spirit, but one to inspire strength' (II Tim. 1.7). The power is already out of hand. God has already gone too far. In vain, we will attempt to restore order, to confine him. This, we will say, is the way that things should be. This, we shall read and write, is the way God is and what he is like. Let everything be done decently and in order – let us not, above all, get carried away. And all the time we are frantically trying to keep things under control, the Spirit of God is unleashed and on the loose, and rushes like wind and fire through any places or people that he chooses. While the religious formulate their doctrines and discuss their liturgies, the Spirit of God is causing havoc, whipping up power and truth and peace and freedom in the places where life is – on the terraces, in the television studios, in politics and social concern, in the Third World, in human rights, in movements for justice and peace. It is in that context that we rejoice when the miracles begin again, the healings, the prophesying, the tongues. As men and women release the inhibitions that bind them to isolation, as they open up, then, whether inside the churches, or way outside them, in the back streets, in the pubs, in tiny offices, they will re-discover the power and the freedom.

The image of the Spirit of 'wind' is the most powerful and accurate of all. It was a driving wind through the Jerusalem room, it was the breath of Jesus on the night of the resurrection. And, as the writer of the Fourth Gospel points out, there is more to wind than that: 'The wind blows where it wills; you hear the sound of it, but you do not know where it comes from, or where it is going' (John 3.8). That is the Spirit – invisible, noisy, its effects strewn behind it, impossible to pin down. To control it is a lost cause; our only hope is to catch up with it. To be taken over by it is a traumatic experience, like being born again. It whips you around and faces you in new directions. 'You ought not to be astonished then when I tell you that you must be born over again: flesh can give birth only to flesh, it is spirit that gives birth to spirit' (3.6–7). And once the take-over has occurred, you become a free spirit: 'Do you not know that your body is a shrine of the indwelling Holy Spirit, and the Spirit is God's gift to you?' (I Cor. 6.19). Just as God is man, so the Spirit makes man alive with him. The experience of the Spirit is not to be defined or confined – it is by nature unpredictable. If something can be organized, foreseen, if its effects are predictable, if we know where it will take us, what it will make us do, it is probably not a movement of the Spirit. Which is why organized religion, for example, leaves the Holy Spirit very little room for manouvre. As ever, the take-over is not a prize for the religious elite, it is a genuine, totally human experience which occurs when humans open themselves enough to let it happen. The very first image in the Bible is of a formless earth, surrounded by total darkness, and suddenly across the surface of the waters, a howling wind or is it, as one can translate it,' 'the Spirit of God hovering'? (Gen. 1.2).

The Spirit is the impact of the religious experience on man, and its overflow. It is the world's conscience, defined by the death and resurrection of Jesus. It is the relation between theology and personal experience, it inspires (literally 'in-spires' with breath and wind) man to become truly personal, and no longer a slave to conventional repetition. Its true evidence is in the lives and attitudes of human beings. Probably far more important than the 'gifts' of the Spirit, are what Paul elsewhere calls the 'harvest' of the Spirit, its results, what we really expect to see left behind in its wake. The gifts may impress for a while, they may be good for dinner-time conversation, but the real fruit of the Spirit is undiscussable and indestructible. These are the things for which we truthfully strive, these are the things we long to see behind the eyes of others, these are the things which we want to believe are the ultimate realities; and they are 'love, joy, peace, patience, kindness, goodness, fidelity, gentleness and self-control. There is no law dealing with such things as these' (Gal. 5.22–23). If the Spirit does not result in these, the Spirit was never there. If it leaves behind nothing else but these, it was the true Spirit of God.

Outside the first church of which I ever had pastoral charge, on the evening of my induction, stood a small boy from the surrounding estate. 'Are you the new Vicar?' he asked, and when I said that I was, he went on, 'Are you a *kind* Vicar?' It is the fruit, the harvest of the Spirit, that the world wants to see. No phoney religious substitute will do.

I cannot deny that in discussing the Holy Spirit, we move out of the area of what is strictly reasonable. Even at the level of the New Testament, it is where we move from the academic to the experiential. A so-called 'radical' theology may reduce all the academic points it likes, one may rephrase all the dogmatic terms in the book, and the more conservative will leap up in alarm and accuse us of reducing the faith to nothing, and, with all this talk of human experience and values, of being no more than a humanist. But unlike the humanist, the grown-up Christian is interpreting his own experience, and not simply confirming what has been told him. If an experience proves something to be ultimately true for me, then it is for me religious experience. No amount of psychological analysing, however true in the technical sense, will deny the nature of the experience. It would be as foolish as explaining away a scrambled egg to the point of saying that a scrambled egg *as such* does not exist, when you have just eaten one. And this seems to me the sum total of the Spirit's work – the transition from philosophy to experience. The presence of the Spirit is the realization that the religious nature of man's experience is unforgettable. The Christ-event is the one event in history that altered humanity and its perception of itself. The individual's own experiential, existential Spirit-event, as it might be called, his re-birth, is the radical alteration of his own life, his own revision of his own self-perception. It is radical because it is an alteration of his context, of where he perceives himself to be, out of finitude into infinity, out of shallowness into depth, out of confusion about himself into integrity. He begins to see that the value of his personality is greater than the sum total of his experiences. It is the beginning of response to the sense of God as love, and moreover as sacrificial love as demonstrated in Jesus. The Spirit is the Spirit of both God and Jesus asserting itself into our present experience, and leading us to the higher ground.

A man's spirit is the man in action, the whole man and the real man which we know not by what he thinks he is or says of himself, but by what he does. A person is like his behaviour and not what he thinks his behaviour ought to be. He is what he is as a result of how he has re-acted to other people and how they have reacted to him. This constitutes the spirit of a person. The Spirit of God is precisely the same. The Spirit *is* the work of the Spirit, it is God's behaviour, it is how we tell what he is like. It is the context in which we live, it bridges dogma and experience, it is the meeting place between the ground of our being and the experiential knowledge of myself. It may achieve all that the early believers claim for it, because it is life. The highest ideals of humanity appear inevitably unfulfillable. We do our best. And we are still left with the ideal that ideals can be fulfilled. The teaching of the Spirit is that man's ideal is God's real. The work of the Spirit is the intrusion of this reality into human experience. The Christian will say, 'I will grant you all that you say about the terms I use, I will expand them, discuss them, if necessary replace them, but you will not deny me the living experience that provoked them.'

The coming of the Spirit is when we indulge in the Christ-event and its significance. And once experienced, there is no real denying. The fruit of the Spirit is not simply a goal to be achieved, but the very reason why we do not deny. Why abandon love, and joy and peace in exchange for nothing? The reality of the Spirit is as evident as the smile on the face of a woman who has borne the child. The Spirit gives birth to the concrete reality of our sense of God in a suffering world.

To this point, we have discussed nothing other than or more than what we mean by the nature of God. I have approached the nature of God in three ways: one as a sense of the Other in the universe, ultimately revealed as love; one as the historical figure of Jesus displaying the nature of God in utterly human terms; and then as a free and powerful Spirit inspiring our experience. I have approached God in these three ways for the obvious reason that they correspond to the versions of God which Christians traditionally define as the Trinity. I do not frankly feel that the concept of God as Trinity is a particularly useful one, or worth spending a great deal of time on. But I am also anxious that it should not be a stumbling-block. I used to have a friend who tried to work it out on his fingers – 'Three into one, one into three! It's no good, it won't go.' The three approaches to the nature of God are convenient, that is all. But I might just as easily have divided, for example, God the Creator from God the Father, and made four approaches, or the Jesus of history from the Christ of faith, and made five. Or I could collate the Christ of faith with the Spirit and made four approaches again. And I could lump that last combination with Creator and make a Trinity again. In other words, it is all rather arbitrary, and a matter for our convenience, and says very little about the nature of God. Nobody seriously believes that there are three gods in one, or that God is divided into three.

But the idea of Trinity, or at least the idea of several faces or aspects of God, does spring from two truths. First, that the concept of God, for all we have said, remains so vast that we cannot see him in any one image, we cannot take him in with just one blink of the eye. The whole of God is love in creation, the whole of God is Jesus, God was in Christ reconciling the world to himself, God is also spirit. We never have enough to describe him. Of course there is one God, but we cannot count him. There are so many faces, aspects, always expanding. The threefold formula of Father, Son and Spirit just about enables us to cope, but do not suppose that God is limited by it. Indeed, part of the point of the formula is to convey that he is not.

And, second, a threefold formula also implies that though we are only considering one God, we are not positing a divine figure poised in splendid isolation. The God that we begin to sense has within its nature something about persons, about love, about relationship, about community. God is being perceived in Christian experience not as passive, but as acting and reacting, as moving, inter-relating. A parable of God as a kind of family – of Father, Son and Spirit – does not, I am sure, bear any remote resemblance to anything in reality, but it does point up the truth about God in relationship which we might never otherwise comprehend.

And it is, of course, all one: the Creator, the Father, the Ground of our Being, the 'there must be something', Love, the God in everything, the wild-eyed Galilean peasant gathering his friends, the man dying, the sensation of his being still alive, the spirit of truth accusing and defending us, the wind whipping us up, the peace settling on us, the God, the Christ, the Spirit that we find in holding out our hands to another human soul. Turn your eyes and it is there.

In 'The Waste Land', T. S. Eliot combines the story of two disciples walking to Emmaus and finding the risen Jesus walking alongside them with a story that came out of an Antarctic expedition that when the party was counted, there was always one more than there ought to be.

> Who is the third who walks always beside you?
> When I count, there are only you and I together
> But when I look ahead up the white road
> There is always another one walking beside you
> Gliding wrapt in a brown mantle, hooded

I do not know whether a man or a woman
– But who is that on the other side of you?[3]

When I was ordained, one of my dearest friends, who knew my passion for Eliot, and a few other things about me as well, sent me a telegram. It said nothing about congratulations or good wishes for the future. It simply said '*But who is that on the other side of you?*' Such was the springboard of Christian faith, and it is also the spur to faith in action, to the nature of the Christian style of living.

FOUR

All You Need is Love?

So much for theology. There is a point where theology has to stop and living has to begin. The temptation with theology as with all speculation, indeed with all academic disciplines, is that it becomes a game for those who like to play it and which carries them further and further away from real life. Theology is rooted in real life, and the sooner it is back there being applied, the better. What we are seeking to do is find a truthful way of living, truthful in the sense that it is true to what we know of ourselves and our world. Thus all we need is enough theology to live by. Anything more is for the game-players. One of the early church's first games was, 'Does the Spirit come from the Father *and* the Son? Or just from the Father?' Bring on the others. 'How many angels can you get on the head of a pin?' 'How many children had Lady Macbeth?' Who cares?

There comes a point where we have observed enough and rationalized enough to provide us with a dream in whose light we may turn existence into something more like life. In exploring the nature of God and the Christian belief, I concede we may already have gone too far. What we have essentially is a sense of God innate in man which precedes the questions about him. That sense pervades everything and appears to be in some way personal and loving. God, in fact, broke through the distortion that divides us from him, expressed his whole being in the human life of Jesus of Nazareth, who lived, loved, taught, healed, was finally executed. His life was apparently of such power that death could not condition him either, and his followers were overwhelmed with a sensation that he was alive. It is a sensation that believers have shared through the generations since. Their belief is vindicated and the world continually disturbed by the unfettered Spirit of God which makes the presence of God felt whenever and wherever it chooses. So where does that leave us? To live by?

The central belief appears to me to be that the God/mankind barrier is smashed. Whichever face of God you care to look at, what this set of propositions offers is a total re-thinking of the God/mankind relationship. This is more than a communication between the two, it is rather a sharing, a co-worker situation. The more traditional religious relationship of abject man crawling before mighty God does not make any sense at all within the Christian framework of thought. (The attitude is marvellously parodied by the Monty Python team in a school prayer: 'O God, you are so great – we are all very impressed down here, I can tell you.') God has become man, and there is no back-tracking. Any form of religion that goes back to the relationship of distance is less than Christian. Indeed, what Christian belief signals is nothing less than the end of religion in its accepted sense, in the sense of religious dependence. The power and the glory has passed to us, along with the responsibilities. We must resist all temptation to indulge in dependency exercises, or to reduce our genuine religious experience to credal statements or organizations. We are free to make valid critiques of the behaviour of the pious without fear of blasphemy – the violence, the intolerance and the dogmatism that has littered the history of what has passed for Christianity. The greatest blasphemy, the breaking of the God/mankind barrier, is completed, and once that truth is grasped, man finds his new freedom. 'If you dwell within the revelation I have brought, you are indeed my disciples: you shall know the truth, and the truth shall set you free ... If the Son sets you free, you will indeed be free' (John 8.32, 36).

So while the Christian faith explores the nature of God, the nature of mankind and the relation between them, the Christian life is for the individual the quest for the ability to stand free. If the truth is that God is man, how do I as man live my life in such a way that will express that truth, not in order to impress people, but because that way of life will harmonize, accord with the truth

I have discovered? If the truth does not make sense of my life, it is not a truth worth knowing. Can this truth, as opposed to other propositions, religious or otherwise, that the world offers, help me to cut through the clutter with which I surround myself? Can it enable me to stand upright and free, to know who and what I am, to relate to the world and other people in a way that accords with what I perceive to be the ultimate reality, the true nature of things? The individual quest, it seems to me, is for a personal maturity, an integrity, that will at least make me proud to be who I am. It needs to be a maturity at a psychological level: I need to find a way above and through my childish greed, or my uncontrollable anger, or whatever it happens to be that drags me down and back from the person I wish to be. It needs to be a maturity at a social level: I need to be able to cope in a sensible way with the boring, irritating person, or to see myself manipulating others for my own ends, or whatever other hang-ups I have about my dealings with other people. And I need to find maturity at, for want of a better word, a spiritual level, at a level where I am at peace with myself, and so adequate, mature enough to live a life that not only fulfils me but those who share space with me.

And these needs I know I share with other human beings. Thus what I am really asking for in my quest for maturity is that I should become more human. There is no greater ambition for me, since God became human, and it is thus to him I strive. What the Jesus-event offers is the conviction that to be fully human is not only desirable, but possible. What we as individuals are striving for is the maturity that is the by-product of becoming truly human, of discovering true humanity. It is precisely this true humanity that Christian belief defines. It is indeed Christianity above all which can make it happen. The true humanity will finally be something that we have in common, it will eventually draw us together. It will not only give maturity to my own striving, but make me aware of the others on the same quest. Thus Paul writes to Ephesus: 'We shall all at last attain to the unity inherent in our faith and our knowledge of the Son of God – to mature manhood, measured by nothing less than the full stature of Christ. We are no longer to be children, tossed by the waves and whirled about by every fresh gust of teaching ... No, let us speak the truth in love, so shall we fully grow up into Christ' (Eph. 4.13–15). Yes, that is it, that is what I want. I want to be Christ when I grow up. Just give me the clue, hand me the key.

The clue, the key, has in fact been there all the time. When we sensed God, we were aware of him most clearly at points of human love. The most significant 'signal of transcendence' came to light at such points of love, moments of gratitude, compassion. We came to sense that what was there at the centre of the universe, in the ground of our being was Love itself, that it was benign and loving towards us. In such a context, the very existence of Jesus is itself an act of love. If he was the abdication of God, then he was himself a demonstration of God's love for us: 'God loved the world so much that he gave his only Son ...' (John 3.16). The earthly life and character of Jesus was itself a definition of human love. Out of love sprang the healings, the miracles, the teaching. Much of the teaching is about love, defining it in terms of behaviour in the parables, and extending its scope and meaning. 'Love your enemies; do good to those who hate you; bless those who curse you; pray for those who treat you spitefully ... If you love only those who love you, what credit is that to you?' (Luke 6.27–28, 32). His life was a practical demonstration of human love, and his death was its climax. At the opening of the section of his Gospel leading up to the crucifixion, John writes: 'He had always loved his own who were in the world, and now he was to show the full extent of his love' (John 13.1). The first Christians quickly came to see his death as an act of sacrificial love for them and for the world: 'the Son of God who loved me and gave himself up for me' (Gal. 2.20). The power that raised him from the dead is the love inherent in God and in Jesus's own life. The Spirit is then presented to man as a loving gift. The highest, the best, the most treasured of the gifts of the Spirit is love. 'The higher gifts are those you should aim at ... I will show you the best way of all ... There are three things that last for ever; faith, hope and love; but the greatest of them all is love. Put love first' (I Cor. 12.31; 13.13–14.1). The first, and most important of the fruits of the Spirit is love. In other words, the massive implication of the whole of Christian belief is that love is central. And more than that, the implication is also that we are loved, that we are the object of love, that we are accepted and acceptable to the universe. And where we failed to be acceptable, that is where Jesus's death and resurrection made us so. We became loved because he was loved. Our freedom is based on the premise that 'there is no condemnation for those who are united with Christ Jesus' (Rom. 8.1). The basic premise of the Christian faith is that we are already loved and accepted, that 'no less than the trees and the stars, you have a right to be here'. They say that a child who has not been loved will never know how to offer love itself. So it is that only when we feel loved, ultimately loved, by the universe, by the ground of our being, do we have the confidence to offer love to others. To be capable of love, we need to be in touch with the reality that ultimately everything is love. The clue, the key, is love. It is learning to love that will mature us and free us. If I had to express in one phrase what Christianity is actually about, I would say it is about loving and being loved. And by an amazing coincidence, that is exactly what I, as a human being, want it to be.

Back in the heady sixties, there was much talk of love, and also peace. The Beatles' song 'All you need is love', though not the most imaginative of their compositions, nevertheless stands now for a whole generation. A whole counter-culture strangely united Eastern and Western thought in its search for love. In the West, at least, it arose as a reaction to the commercial and material boom that followed the war, and frankly the boom was itself a cushion and a security for young people to indulge in. In these days of unemployment and poverty, we cannot afford the luxury of rebellion with love and peace. But for a few sunny years, love appeared to rule – at the Woodstock festival, in San Francisco, where you had to go with flowers in your hair, behind the badges declaring 'Make love, not war'. The whole music scene, the arts, the politics were alive with love. The caring professions attracted thousands of young people; international relations boomed. Love showed itself in physical contacts, in a new openness about sex, in the colours and songs of the city.

We may never know 'which came first', but the Christian faith found a home and some hope in all that. Out of Boenhoffer's 'religionless Christianity' and Tillich's 'ground of our being', a radical theology was born that blended perhaps too easily, too unquestioningly with the times. It came to a head in Britain with Bishop Robinson's *Honest to God*, which mildly but to brutal effect destroyed the 'old man in the sky' image of God, posited Jesus as 'the man for others', opened up what had been traditional ethics. In America the slogan 'God is dead' became a valid Christian theological position. And love, as in the culture around it, was everything. Brian Epstein, the Beatles' manager, was quoted as saying: 'When you have said "all you need is love", you have said everything.' A whole new community of young Christians would agree.

Now, of course, we all know very much better. We were warned at the time by the cynics that the dream would turn sour, that we may love now, but pay later. And traditional Christians were telling us that all we were doing to the faith was reducing it, downgrading it, cheapening it. We were reducing God to mere love: we were saying to achieve him, we had only to love each other. Christian truth was about far more important things than love. It is a convincing charge, it succeeded in making the radical Christian movement appear pretty silly. Training colleges for the churches returned to normal, no longer concerned with the trivia of love, more intent on the deeper things of the faith. This, of course, happened all the easier as the culture around collapsed, as a new generation counter-rebelled and became conservative and well-dressed. Commercial interests, particularly in hard drugs, took obscene advantage and corrupted and literally destroyed a generation, and supported, to their shame, by academics who should have known better. The forces of law and order moved in and restored the *status quo*. They don't bother with love and peace and tolerance in California now. The ageing hippy is the laughed at symbol of a foolish and lost culture. And the Christian faith does not wish to be part of that.

We are speaking of fifteen years ago and more. The counter-arguments have held sway, politically, culturally, religiously, ever since. Only now that the cracks are beginning to appear, only now as the social fabric built without love appears to shake, only now can we perhaps intelligently reassess. We will need at some point to look at the social and political ramifications, but for the moment, let us return to the charge of reducing the faith. The charge, however hard it stuck, is riddled with fallacies, tested by experience or by the Bible. The mistake is not in the reduction of God to love, but in the reduction of love to 'mere love'. You cannot reduce God to 'mere love', because there is no such thing. Love is love, and God is love. It is not a matter of 'only' loving each other. Loving each other is not an easy option; it is the hardest way of all, it is what most human beings sweat most of their lives away trying to learn how to do. Christian truth cannot be about more important things than love, since Christian truth is that there is nothing more important than love. Love is not an easy alternative to real Christian living, it is real Christian living – the easy alternative to love is to retreat to theological discussion, or books or buildings or career structures or spiritual experiences or synods. These are the trivia of Christianity, not love. Love is the one in the middle, the rough one, the deepest thing of the faith, because it is the deepest, most difficult thing of human life. In other words, the time has now come to reinstate love at the centre of the faith, and to stop evading it. It is the one thing, literally the one thing that people expect the Christian to be at least learning how to do. It is time Christians unashamedly started trying to do it again. To do so, love must be returned to the centre of theology and ethics. Radical theology of the sixties reduced nothing to nothing, it put love where the God of love put it. It is the next generation of Christians who have betrayed it, because it was no longer fashionable. But it is precisely because love and peace are no longer fashionable that Christians need to re-assert them.

There is no escaping that to love is the central ethical command of the Christian life. 'I give you a new commandment; love one another as I have loved you, so you are to love one another. If there is this love among you, then all will know that you are my disciples' (John 13.34–35). 'This is my commandment; love one another, as I have loved you. There is no greater love than this, that a man should lay down his life for his friends' (15.12–13). 'I may speak in tongues of men or of angels, but if I am without love, I am a sounding gong or a clanging cymbal . . . if I have no love, I am nothing' (I Cor. 13.1–3).

The biblical case for love is put most strongly in the first letter of John. 'The message you have heard from the beginning is this: that we should love one another . . . The man who does not love is still in the realm of death, for everyone who hates his brother is a murderer . . . It is by this that we know what love is, that Christ laid down his life for us . . . Love must not be a matter of words or talk: it must be genuine and show itself in action . . . Let us love one another, because love is from God . . . Only the man who loves his brother dwells in light.' In the sixties, such words were cheered. We were lucky. Now words like 'love' and their attendants – caring, compassion, concern – are regarded as sloppy, 'wet', unrealistic, idealistic. We live in a age dedicated to cruelty and violence calling itself cold, reasonable pragmatism. The Christian by definition can have none of it. God is love, and love rules, and it is the only key, the only clue, the only route to personal maturity, integrity and peace. The Christian ethic is love. Anything else is not Christian. Christianity is about loving and being loved. It is about nothing else, because there is nothing else. Because it is about God, and he is love, and he is everything.

Thus 'the Pharisees met together and one of their number tested Jesus with this question: "Master, which is the greatest commandment in the law?" He answered "Love the Lord your God with all your heart, with all your soul, with all your mind. That is the greatest commandment. It comes first. The second is like it: Love your neighbour as yourself. Everything in the law and the prophets hangs on these two commandments."' Jesus thus poses the two commands of love, the two aspects of loving. So what does he mean by love for God, and how does it show itself? And what does it mean to love a neighbour as myself? In what sense am I to love myself? What is the shape of love? And how are the loves like each other?

I do not believe that a love for God is something that can be cultivated artificially. No amount of ritual or religious discipline can make a person love God. Love, Christianity, is something that is, as they say, caught rather than taught, and that includes any sense of our loving God. Love for God, as and when it happens, is in response to the love that we feel coming across to us. When we sense that the ground of our being is in fact expressing its love for us, when we become aware that the very existence of Jesus was an act of love towards us, when we feel the glimmers of gratitude that our human frailty has been made acceptable in the universe, as we finally understand that, in a way, we do not have to seek for God, because in love, he has already come seeking us – then with a certain warmth, we begin to find our own individual place in the scheme of things. When I begin to feel loved and accepted for myself, despite all I know of myself, then I find my only response is to turn towards the source of love, to respond, to express my own love into the heart of things. Jesus himself spotted such response in a prostitute who wiped his feet with her hair. 'Her great love proves that her many sins have been forgiven; where little has been forgiven, little love is shown' (Luke 7.47). 'We love', as the first letter of John says, 'because he loved us first' (I John 4.20).

Our love for God is no more or less than the instinctive response to the love we believe he shows to us. And though it may not be cultivated, it does appear within the Christian experience to develop. It does so in progressive stages. The first response to love in the universe is one of security, a feeling that it is all right, that here we belong. It is this that teaches us trust, that makes us less fearful of the world and its future, that it is possible to rest, to let go. It is the beginning of a belief that a God who has shown love to me on such a scale is ultimately to be trusted, a God in whose hands I am safe. I am therefore able to take my own risk with the world and the universe – if he loved it, I may love it: if he embraced it, I may embrace it. I am able to say 'Yes' to the world and to life. I can let go and let God. This is what I understand

Christians to mean by *faith*. It is not a matter of believing six impossible things before breakfast: faith is not asking rational man to behave irrationally, it is rather asking him, in response to love, to relinquish fear about himself and his world, and to place such value on love that he relaxes into trusting them. Faith is the first stuttering response of love to love, its purpose is 'to make life our own . . . Faith gives substance to our hopes, and makes us certain of realities we do not see' (Heb. 10.39–11.1). Faith enables us to say things, do things, go places that we would not otherwise risk.

Such a response to love opens us up and relaxes, but may leave us offering no more to the world than a benign smile and a willingness to travel. At some point in our response, an individual is going to have to commit himself. If this is the true scale of the truth we have discovered and the love we have experienced, then the response that is called for is of a totally committing life-long kind. It is not an attitude to life that one can drift in and out of. This is what one wing of the faith means by a conversion experience – what we must be careful not to do is to limit what we mean by that. It may indeed be a blinding vision on a road to Damascus or at an evangelical rally or on Victoria station, but it may equally well be a conversation with someone, or grown into over a number of years, or a rational decision made alone in a study. What matters is that we feel committed to the thing now – we may not know we have committed ourselves until after we have done so. At some point, each man or woman seeking God finds God seeking him or her, trusts God in faith, and then finds the thing is so important that it demands a response not just of trust, but of commitment. 'All I know is this: once I was blind, now I can see' (John 9.25). It says nothing about my moral state, the quality of my life, merely that I have seen something which cannot be unseen, and in the light of which my life has to be lived because there are no longer any real alternatives. This way of looking at the world and my fellow human beings appears so right that any lesser way appears inconceivable, and it appears so important that it demands the whole of me, all the loving response that I can give. I have one friend who was training to be ordained with me. He decided not to go ahead on the grounds that if there was a God, nothing was more important, and he must mean everything. He was not, my friend said, that important to me, therefore I do not truly believe in him. Once you realize that God, whatever you conceive him to be, has invested everything in you, committed himself totally to you, then the only response, logical and loving, is a total commitment to him. It is about choosing a way of life. This is what I understand Christians to mean by repentance. It has nothing to do with humans crawling abjectly in front of an angry and powerful God, confessing their sins and waving a white flag. That is some other religion, a false one that springs from man's own guilt. Such guilt must not be fed in the name of Christianity. No, repentance is a Greek word, *metanoia*, which means 'changing your mind', turning round, facing in a new direction, deciding to go a different way. It is what the old Prayer Book called 'intending to lead a new life'. Repentance is part of the response to the love of God. It is the stage beyond faith, the stage where love commits itself. Since the crucifixion of Jesus is the image that conveys most vividly the extent and sacrificial nature of God's love, it is when we have caught the truth and power of the cross in particular that we find the love irresistible and commitment unavoidable. Once I have seen what God's love for me cost him in sweat and agony, in the splitting of the godhead and the abdication of his power, that the evil that he absorbed and became on the cross included all my evil, all my weakness, all my frailty, then finally I have no choice. 'Repent', turn round, was the first challenge of Jesus (Mark 1.15). 'Repent', turn round, was the first challenge to the world by the new-born, Spirit-filled community when they were asked 'What are we to do?' (Acts 2.37–38). I defy any human being to truly understand the cross and not to respond with a commitment for life to view the world with those eyes. I try to resist it on grounds of sentimentality, but I have not seen it better expressed than in Isaac Watts's hymn, and I find myself returning to it:

When I survey the wondrous cross
   on which the Prince of glory died,
my richest gain I count but loss,
   and pour contempt on all my pride . . .

Were the whole realm of nature mine,
   that were a present far too small;
Love so amazing, so divine,
   demands my soul, my life, my all.

There are certain brands of the Christian faith which appear to
stop at that point. Once the call to faith and repentance has been
proclaimed and responded to, there is nowhere else to go, and so
we go on repeating it and hope that other people will hear it and
respond, and in their turn join the cycle of perpetual motion.
The result is always a clique of people who meet to go through
the endless process, people who know a great deal about faith and
repentance. They also as a result of endless repetition know a
great deal about manipulating people, and how best to trap them
into the pattern. But the pattern is closed, because it knows about
the maintenance of a cosy experience and not about response to
the love of God. So love for God stops at repentance, and, as a
result, love for the neighbour stops at manipulation. We, on the
other hand, must move into a new stage of love for God. Once
trusting, once committed, it now becomes important that one's
love for God is continually refreshed and renewed, not by repetition, but by becoming more and more open to him. The search
for him which began as something we sensed in his world, becomes a deep experiential enquiry into the meaning of love, to
discover 'what is the breadth and length and height and depth of
the love of Christ, and to know it, though it is beyond knowledge. So may you attain to fullness of being, the fullness of God
himself' (Eph. 3.18-19). Thus the Christian begins, I believe, to
find regular ways of renewing and refreshing both his understanding of God's love and his own love for God, so that the
vision is continually being expanded, so that, having seen, he
now learns to see more, and so trust more and ultimately love

more. This is what I understand Christians to mean by spirituality, or the spiritual life. It has nothing to do with going through motions in obedience to some religious discipline. Pious devotions do not of themselves give any credit to those who perform them, and they are often blasphemous nonsense. But their true purpose is as a means to an end, and they must be battered into shape to suit our ends. If they do not make me love better, they are wasting my time. But with the end firmly in view, the individual soul may seek to reach deeper and deeper into the heart of love, and he must find his own way to do it. It may be a simple pattern of Bible reading and prayer, it may be the saying of an office, it may be a pattern of attendance at Mass, it may be silence, it may also be patterns of meditation and contemplation, it may be deep breathing in the morning air, it may be a programme of reading or listening to music. It probably should be a mixture, a changing pattern of all those things and others too. Clinging to any one of them is probably the surest way to a deadly routine, and the routine becomes an idol. The spiritual pattern may or may not be directly related to, or make specific reference to the Christian faith. The quest, after all, is not to become more religious, but to grow up, to become more human and more loving, so we are prepared to use any means to increase our awareness of love. The sources of our spirituality may be drawn from faiths other than the Christian one or from the secular world which God loves and has made sacred.

But the emphasis must always be on the ends, and the means are found to meet them. And the task is always that of growing, of opening up more and more of myself to the divine love, a continual reaching of my hands towards it. The end, we must remember, is to learn how to love. A genuine spiritual life leads us to that end as we discover new truths about God who is Love itself. We learn, for example, the utter integrity of God, the utter lack of confusion between thought and deed, his unique capacity to practice what he preaches, to be what he says he is. It is this total integrity which the Bible calls 'righteousness' (indeed, one modern translation actually uses the word 'integrity'). As we draw closer to the one point where belief and action are not divided, so we learn how to put what we have found by faith into action with integrity. We learn, in other words, to love. Second, as we draw closer and closer to love as the centre of the universe, and as we truly understand its importance, then other ambitions begin to fall away. We sense for a moment that nothing is nearer to what we want than to love and be loved, and all the other wants and desires, cravings and expectations from life assume their proper place, fall into perspective. Our chief ambition becomes to love. And thirdly, and ironically, the more I love God, and the more I discover his love for me, the higher value I may safely put on myself. I met someone again recently whom I knew to be keen on transcendental meditation. She was not a Christian – her meditation was Eastern-based with a strong element of twentieth-century secularism. I asked her if she still practised it. 'Oh yes,' she replied, 'I still need to know who I am.'

God is the ground of our being. As we reach deeper and deeper into him, we are also reaching deeper and deeper into our own souls and personalities. We are indeed literally learning who we are, where we fit, what we want. Ultimately, we begin to put the same value on ourselves that God does, we come, in a true sense, to love ourselves. In seeking to 'love God', we have been learning to love love itself, since God is love, and as we love love, we open ourselves to love touching us. We can expose our love without the fear of being trampled on. In other words, the whole process of finding God to be love, to believe that we are passionately loved in Christ, striving to love God, the progressive sequence of faith, repentance and the spiritual life is all geared to just one end, the true discovery of the self, a true value on the self which gives us, in a way that nothing else can, the confidence to love, and to love not just ideas but our fellow travellers. Love is full of risks and pain, as any lover will tell you. There is apparent safety in avoiding love, since then we cannot be hurt. 'I am a rock, I am an island, for a rock feels no pain, and an island never cries' (Paul Simon). What the Christian faith uniquely offers, I believe, is such a high view of the true self that it becomes confident enough to take the risk, in the certain knowledge that the pain of love is the only route to real life, that crucifixion is the only way to resurrection. The false selves, the phoney dreams we have of ourselves, may be left behind. It is precisely the pain of love, the cross, that we may risk picking up. The disciple 'must leave self behind . . . he must take up his cross . . . What will a man gain by winning the whole world, at the cost of his true self?' (Luke 9.23–26). The Christian is the one who lets himself go, because he can afford to do so, because he knows his true self, and knows it to be ultimately loved. The trick, and it is the crucial one, the one that really matters, is how, claiming that I love God, I can learn to love my neighbour, and I mean by that, love my neighbour as myself.

Thus a love of God, a love of love, a proper love of self are the only solid basis from which love of others can begin. This is the Christian ethic and the Christian life. In the Christian context, all personal ethics and morality are measured by the test of love as we have already experienced it. To such loving we were born. In a sense, this ethic of individual love is the core of Christianity – this is the central point of any apologetic for the faith. The matters of belief that precede it are there to make human love possible, all that follows is to enable us to love better. Nothing is more important than the love of human beings for one another; God has said it and indulged in it, there is no higher authority.

The ethic of love stands in direct contrast to the morality into which human beings naturally slide. That is why 'metanoia', repentance, is necessary. Without trust in love at the heart of things, without having the resurrection following the cross, without the confidence in mankind that love gives, we naturally think that the only way people will behave towards each other with any degree of acceptance is by obeying rules and laws laid down to order our lives. This is the natural human way. When things appear to be crumbling, the frightened and unconfident will always appeal to law, order, authority, discipline. If only, we feel, we could have a set of rules which everybody followed, all would be peace and harmony. The truth is, of course, that in society after society, law on its own has failed to work. The Old Testament is the story of a nation committed to law who, by New Testament times, were burdened with the guilt that the law provoked, and who were governed by pious hypocrites who kept the law, but who had forgotten what it was for. The prohibition of alcohol in the United States produced a level of addiction and drunkenness unknown before. Every attempt to clamp down with discipline produces a backlash of anarchy. It is a mug's game. And ultimately every free human spirit that God has made is going to bounce back with 'Who says?' Who are you to determine which way I shall live? The way of law only creates guilt if we fail to keep it. 'The good which I want to do, I fail to do; but what I do is the wrong which is against my will' (Rom. 7.19). The law, authority, discipline is an attractive snare, but there is no way out once the trap closes behind you. 'Who is there to rescue me out of this body doomed to death?' (7.24). Christians will reject all attempts to impose authority on them. For the Christian, there is only one authority, and that is the vision of Jesus Christ that he has seen in the created world and in the love between human beings. Nothing less must ever claim his allegiance or obedience.

It must be frankly admitted that some Christians appear more enthusiastic to live by rules and impose them than many secular people. Those Christians are quite simply wrong. They have not yet learned the confidence in God and in themselves that will allow them to be free of law. It has always been a problem for the Christian community; one of the earliest rows, between Peter and Paul, arose because Peter thought that Gentiles, once converted to Christ, ought to take on the Jewish law, including circumcision. Mutilation rather, Paul called it, and thankfully his view prevailed. Similarly, the Christian community today is burdened with those who have not quite grasped the freedom of the God-become-man, and still believe they can impose regulations on the personal lives of others. I am afraid we just have to ignore them, and hopefully lead them by example to a better way.

There is really no ducking it. The way of love is opposed to the natural way of law. 'You are no longer under law, but under the grace of God' (Rom. 6.14). 'We are discharged from the law, to serve God in a new way, the way of the spirit' (7.6). We are committed 'not to a system of earth-bound rules, but to the power of a life that cannot be destroyed ... The earlier rules are cancelled as impotent and useless, since the law brought nothing to perfection; and a better hope is introduced' (Heb. 7.16–19). Whatever ethic we contrive for the Christian faith, whatever we perceive as its moral dimension, it will have nothing whatever to do with law, rules, authority or discipline.

Or, at least, only in one sense. The way of love is itself obedience to the ultimate law in the universe. The most heinous crime in the history of the world was the murder of Jesus, and no law in the world could have prevented it. The ultimate law is the one that took him to the cross – the law of love. Thus the way of love is not a rejection of law, it is obedience to the only law that matters. Jesus maintained: 'Do not suppose that I have come to abolish the law ... I did not come to abolish, but to complete' (Matt. 5.17). He then goes on to point out the futility of a law against murder, if you can do nothing about the anger and frustration that provokes it, if you do nothing to create peace; and the futility of a law against adultery – you might just as well pass a law against physical desire. And so, with Paul as the champion, the Christian community decided very early on that it was love that mattered. 'He who loves his neighbour has satisfied every claim of the law. For the commandments "You shall not commit adultery, you shall not kill, you shall not steal, you shall not covet" and any other commandment there may be, are all summed up in the one rule, "Love your neighbour as yourself" ... The whole law is summed up in love' (Rom. 13.9–10). Thus if anyone is under the impression that the Christian life is about submitting to any other authority than love, or consists of adherence to a set of rules other than the law of love, he has been severely misled. And if any man-made rule, however pious its intention, does not meet others in love, it is not to be supported by Christians.

So how do we test that? How do we know what is loving? We will know, I think, partly instinctively, as a result of what we have seen. If we have sensed God aright, if we have seen the incarnation, death and living of Jesus aright, if we have locked into the Spirit aright, then to some degree we will recognize love when we see it, and we will sniff out phoney substitutes. If our testing of love seems to be failing us, then perhaps we need to remember how we first found it and defined it. That is a process which the Christian will go through time and again. We will know also through the illustration, example of love by others. The Bible, Christian history, the world around us, is full of love in action. Paul is probably the one who has given us the most well-known description of it, and it cannot be far from definitive. 'Love is patient; love is kind and envies no one. Love is never boastful, nor conceited, nor rude; never selfish, not quick to take offence. Love keeps no score of wrongs: does not gloat over other men's sins, but delights in the truth' (I Cor. 13.4–6). 'It is always ready to excuse, to trust and to hope, and to endure whatever comes' (13.7 – Jerusalem Bible).

Thus we can test and recognize Christian love to some extent. At the risk of seeming pedantic about something so all-consuming, so ultimately beautiful, I think it is recognized in three main ways, that it has these three main characteristics, and may be tested and recognized in these three broad areas.

First, Christian love will be about sensitivity and awareness. In the process of Christian believing, mankind has to learn how to open himself, be sensitive to his world, to be aware of God within it. He has to be in the world with nerve-ends exposed and antennae switched on. He takes risks with himself. Love calls upon him to open up in the same way to and for other people, to take the same risks in approaching them, knowing that each other individual has his or her own nerve-ends. It is reaching out to them in the same way as we reached out to God, it is allowing ourselves to be taken over by them as we were by God. In developing such sensitivity, we seek the ground of their being which we share with them, and so being able to find the God and the self in them, to recognize Christ in them. It will mean seeing the other person whole and not simply defined as 'other' or as an extension of oneself. Then we can take the risk of allowing our own life to be trampled into. It is to do with opening up, finding the warmth and excitement of knowing and understanding another human soul, which is like mine, but also shiningly different. Love will then know what lies behind the eyes, it will recognize need when it sees it, and so it will be capable of compassion. Learning to love like this, to be sensitive to others, aware of their being means casting away the false self of inhibition and respectability with which we cloud our social contacts. The handshake keeping the other at arm's length will be replaced by the embrace, holding each other, warm and supporting. It makes us vulnerable, of course, tingling, fearful, entering into other lives, but it is such vulnerability that brings the dead to life. It is in sensitive openness to another soul that I come awake, come alive. We know when we have loved, and when we have failed to do so.

With that degree of openness, of vulnerability, there will of course be pain, bungles, misjudgments, crashes. Which is why Christian love will be recognized, secondly, by its forgiveness. To Jesus, the ability to forgive after the hurt was fundamental to human relationship – again and again 'forgive others the wrong they have done' (Matt. 5.14), an infinite number of times if necessary. Many of the parables are about the ability or inability of people to forgive, people like the elder brother in the story of the Prodigal Son, so locked into the sense of his own righteousness that he is incapable of hearing someone else say 'Sorry'. And, as with openness, the simple reason for the compulsion to forgive is that the Christian is, by definition, one who senses himself to have been forgiven. We did not have to earn the love of God – it is absolutely central that 'Christ died for us while we were yet sinners' (Rom. 5.8); we did not have to wait until we were good enough. So, in the same way, others should not have to earn our love. The same pattern of repentance and acceptance will be the characteristic of the Christian's love for another, as the way that ultimately leads to peace. Indeed, Jesus goes so far as to hint that our right to be forgiven by God is dependent on our willingness to forgive each other. Thus, coupled with the propensity to forgive, Christian love will reject utterly any idea that people should be treated as they deserve, and in particular the notion of revenge. The Christian will attempt to meet another in his need, not weighing what the other may or may not deserve, just as the Christian himself was met in his need. And so revenge

– the attitude of having what is one's due – is not on offer. 'Do not repay wrong with wrong, or abuse with abuse; on the contrary, retaliate with blessing' (I Peter 3.9). 'Never pay back evil for evil ... Do not seek revenge, but leave a place for divine retribution ... If your enemy is hungry, feed him; if he is thirsty, give him a drink; by doing this you will heap five coals on his head. Do not let evil conquer you, but use good to defeat evil' (Rom. 12.17–21). In short, in the Christian book, two wrongs never make a right. There is no case for giving as good as you get. Love is about forgiveness, grudges not held, about not retaliating. Better crucifixion. There may be a rough human justice about revenge, about 'an eye for an eye, a tooth for a tooth', it may give a passing satisfaction to have got your own back. But it is specifically unChristian, and has no place in love.

And thirdly, Christian love ethics are distinguished by their ability to allow personal freedom. Outstanding in Jesus's own life was his refusal to condition anyone, his willingness to allow people to be themselves, his refusal to force them to change, his love for them as they were. It is from the personal freedom that he allows me that I am able to find him. I am not dragooned into submission. I remain free at any point to reject him and all that I have come to believe. Many of his harshest words were for those of the pious who revelled in judging other people – so 'pass no judgment, and you will not be judged. For as you judge others, so you will yourselves be judged ... Why do you look at the speck of sawdust in your brother's eye, with never a thought for the great plank in your own?' (Matt. 7.1–3). Above all, criticizing others, telling others what they should or should not do, restricting their freedom, is simply not your business. 'Who are you to pass judgment on someone else's servant?' (Rom. 14.4). So those, and particularly Christians, who set themselves up as moral guardians and intend to interfere with other people's moral decisions should be ashamed of themselves and frankly shut up. If such people who put such energy into criticizing and judging others were to put half of it into constructive loving, the world would be a better place. The Christian ethic is permissive in that it permits people to be. What used to be called disparagingly the 'permissive society' was far nearer to the spirit of the New Testament than today's pious nonsense. Personal freedom is sacrosanct, and there is a great deal of 'live and let live' about Christian morality. In this century, it has taken psychology and therapy of various kinds to break through the restrictions to freedom that puritans have imposed, often in the name of religion. Christianity is on the side of therapy, of setting prisoners free. The prayer written by Frederick Perls, a developer of Gestalt therapy, expresses the Christian view of personal freedom: 'I do my thing, and you do your thing. I am not in this world to live up to your expectations. And you are not in this world to live up to mine. You are you, and I am I. And if, by chance, we find each other, it's beautiful. If not, it can't be helped.' God introduced himself to Moses by the name 'I AM WHO I AM', that is, utter integrity (Ex. 3.14). Paul, on assessing what God has done for him, reflects, 'By God's grace, I am what I am' (I Cor. 15.10). The least we can do is permit others, too, to be themselves.

The Christian love-ethic will ring true to what we know of God, who is love, it will accept love as the prime law of the universe, and it will be characterized by sensitivity and awareness of others, by a continual willingness to forgive, and by an insistence on the personal freedom of others. It all comes as no surprise, since it is, in Christ, exactly the way that we have been treated by God. All we have to do is behave towards others not only 'as you would like them to treat you' (Matt. 7.12), but as God has behaved towards us. He became so sensitive to us, so aware of us, so open and vulnerable to us that he became one of us and got crucified in the process: he has forgiven us so completely and goes on forgiving us so continually that there is now 'nothing in death or life . . . nothing in all creation that can separate us from the love' (Rom. 8.38–39) – there is nothing I can do so vile that he cannot and will not forgive: and he has given me total personal freedom to be who I am. All I have to do is treat others the same way. 'In a word, accept one another, as Christ accepted us' (Rom. 15.7).

It is all very self-evident. All the more surprising then to find how much of what has passed for Christian morality is in fact nothing of the kind – Christians who bring up children on a reward-and-punishment system without a qualm, those who will happily ban anyone from doing anything if it is not to their taste. I take as a particular example sexual ethics, not because it is the only morality that matters – it may indeed be the least important – but because it does present the morality of personal relation-ships in a heightened form. In this area, so-called Christian views have, in a distorted form, done more harm than anywhere else. And it may present us with specific examples of how a genuine love-ethic might work in practice. Let us then set about the con-struction, or at least, the bare bones of a sexual ethic based on the principles of Christian love as we have found them.

In the first instance, sex is an animal drive and appetite which we share with the rest of God's animal creation, so there is no need to be coy or squeamish about it. There is also no point in denying its existence or behaving as if it didn't exist. But in human terms, it is also the most profound and exhilarating way in which one human being shows love or care for another. Because it is so profound, and therefore so sensitive an area, we must approach it with all the moral dimension that we have built. Each sexual encounter or potential sexual encounter is part of a relationship; it does not exist as a physical action in isolation. You cannot divorce the sexual act from the relationship and the place of sex within it. Thus if we are going to be sensitive and aware in our loving at this point, we will be aware of what the other person thinks of the relationship, feels about it, and how he or she sees sex within it. Awareness will ask questions like, 'What does the other person want or need?', as opposed to 'What do I think the other person ought or ought not to feel?' It will be, as ever, about response to love, and so will run risks – the risk of being rejected, the risk of feeling guilty, the risk of making a mistake. It will take such risks out of love for the other person – it will not wish to manipulate another person, it will not wish to gratify appetite without knowing the other's needs and feelings, it will not lie to another, it will not trample all over his or her feelings, it will not deliberately set up a situation in which another may be hurt or rejected. Nor will its first concern be to keep our own moral hands clean. To refuse to make love may in some circumstances be damaging. A Christian sexual ethic based on sensitivity and awareness will be one by which people tread with love, with honesty and with care, so that their mistakes cause as little pain as possible. Like all mature morality, there will be no rules to help achieve it – it must be simply met and cared about at each point. Thus sexual experiences will be selfish if they are approached with pre-conceptions – if you have already made up your mind that sex should only happen in the bedroom, or in the evening, or in the context of marriage. Sexual morality will be for the Christian far more demanding than that, far more concerned with the other's experience than one's own principles, and ultimately far more loving. Christianity does not take the easy option route to sexual love, either. Sensitive, aware sex can and does take place outside the context of marriage, and crass, insensitive sex can and does take place within it, often especially within it.

Christian sex morality will likewise have within it the ability to forgive and to be forgiven. For some reason, it seems to have got into our consciousness that sexual mistakes are less forgive-able than others. We are often cruel and clumsy in all the aspects of our loving, and God forgives us. He does so in the area of sex, too. And as a result, we forgive each other for selfishness and stupidity in our use of sex. Sexual jealousy is, for example, for the Christian forgiveable. Making love when we did not really want to, or when it hurt someone else, does not mean that a relationship is utterly broken. In our scheme of things, we may forgive each other and restore the broken relationship. We accept the sexual mistakes and failures of someone else because we love them, whether it be a trust broken, or a foolish infatuation, or an unloving approach. Nobody condones mistakes, selfishness of any kind, but the Christian ethic is undoubtedly that all sin is forgiveable.

And, third, the Christian sex ethic will allow the other person to be the sexual person he or she is. It is built in that we do not judge the sexual activities, priorities or needs of somebody else – indeed, it may be more important to speak of meeting needs.

But I have no right to judge the decisions of any other person in matters of sex, whether it be my spouse, the postman or 'young people today'. Hence some practical ramifications will be things like: the Christian will be against all discrimination against homosexuals, who have exactly the same right to love and be loved as heterosexuals, and Christians will rejoice in all loving relationship, whatever sexual orientation; the Christian will allow the woman the supreme right to decide what she does or does not do with her own body, especially in the matters of abortion, and will not interfere with absolute theories either way; Christian parents will allow their children to decide for themselves if and when they wish to take sensible contraceptive precautions, since children should not be encouraged to adopt second-hand morality, but must learn to find their own way.

Sexual love is, finally, for the Christian, the most beautiful, free, loving way in which human beings find each other. It is tingling with excitement, it is aesthetically attractive, it is, perhaps above all, fun. We love to make love, we love to talk about it, we love to find each other through it.

That all seems to me a perfectly sensible, grown-up, caring approach to sex that is quite consistent with, and indeed based on what Christians have learned of the love of God. Yet this is a classic case of where what passes for Christian morality seems to indicate an ethic that leads in exactly the opposite direction. Why should this be? The answer is not all that difficult to find, based on a series of misunderstandings and inadequacies.

Clearly, in the first instance, a puritan sex-ethic is still with the illusion that morality is governed by rules, by law. Thus their first instinct is to introduce rules for sex that will make the whole thing safer. What they regrettably forget is that it takes most of the love out of it, too, because rules make sensitivity and awareness redundant. But they will also appeal to the Bible for justification of their rules. They do so chiefly because they have misunderstood the word 'porneia', which for some reason most English translations read 'fornication', and which is apparently expressly forbidden. 'Fornication' is generally taken to mean 'all sex outside the context of marriage'. In fact, 'porneia' is a word that may only be applied to men (women just cannot commit it, whatever it is) and it means quite specifically 'the act of going to a prostitute', since the Greek word for prostitute is 'porne'. 'Porneia' has an exact meaning, which the New Testament seems to forbid, but whose meaning the puritans have extended without much justification to meet their own needs. In fact, in the context of the New Testament, the most likely activity being forbidden is ritual prostitution, the use of prostitutes in worship, which is obviously difficult to accept by Christian love-standards.

Some problems arise from the New Testament simply because the times have changed. The introduction of contraceptives drastically and obviously changes the whole framework of thought about sex, and gives a context that the Bible simply cannot share. If sex is likely to result in children, it is almost a different activity from one that is highly unlikely to do so. Where once abstaining from sex was a loving thing to do, it is now highly unlikely to be so, since loving will now mean using sensible precautions. Contraception has made it possible for sex to enter the arena of 'homo ludens', it can be now part of the fun and relaxation of human life, and contemporary Christians may rejoice in that in a way that biblical Christians could never understand. Another vastly changed attitude is the position of women. The New Testament still comes from a time when undeniably women were second-class citizens, when they were regarded as adjuncts to men, as their property. Thus to sleep with someone else's wife was quite simply stealing; it was taking his property, it was as bad as taking his ox, or his house, or his car. That is what the Bible means by 'adultery'. Without being dogmatic, I wonder whether it may not be time to assert that people are not objects, that they are not the property of another human being, and that the biblical concept of 'adultery' is now pretty meaningless. This is not to suggest that everybody should make love to other people's wives all the time, but I do think that the Christian love-ethics may call for a rather higher view of persons, a greater emphasis on personal decision-making than seems to have been prevalent in Bible times. And last, much puritanism as opposed to Christian morality arises from that considerable but inexplicable emphasis placed in Christian tradition on sexual sin, which has set up guilts and hang-ups that commonsense has a very difficult job to get through. But get through it we must.

It is important to assert quite unequivocally that I have not suggested for one second that all sexual activity is justified; Christianity does not give sexual carte blanche, and the Bible is quite clear that we must be very careful with our use of freedom. It is therefore very important to accept within the Christian love-ethic, that those who wish to deny sexual love to other people before they themselves are married by a life-long pair-bonding commitment, and those who wish, having made such a commitment, to restrict sexual activity to their partner, are of course perfectly right, and have every right to do so. They must not be mocked, criticized, judged or made to feel inferior by the path that they have chosen. What they in turn must not do is criticize or judge those who have made other decisions about sex, which may be equally responsible, and possibly less cold and more loving. Quite simply, I believe the world would be a happier place if more people adopted the Christian love-ethic. I would be angry if some people were prevented from doing so because a narrow band of Christians gave the impression that sexual ethics were only about following a set of rules which seem to be about forbidding sex in most circumstances. The idea, for example, of a Christian campaigner bringing, say, a court case against a magazine because, for instance, it advocated homosexuality would be, should such a case arise, a total rejection of the Christian love-ethic, a massive piece of personal hypocrisy, and, most important of all, a shameful witness to the love of God. It might give the impression to some homosexuals that they were not able to be Christians. And that would be, quite simply, a lie.

What becomes clear, not only from the discussion of sex, but from the whole pattern of loving and being loved, is that Christian ethics are not in any sense legalistic, but that they are what has come to be known as 'situational'. God did not give us a code, he gave us his Spirit, and it is by the Spirit that we test and decide each moral decision in each situation. There are no short cuts, we really do have to find out for ourselves at each point. The only way to achieve it is to be so close to the nature of love that we learn to recognize it, to know how to handle it, to see when we have made a mess of it. It is a matter of living and loving and growing as we go. All we have to take with us is what God has given us, but that is 'the new nature, which is constantly being renewed in the image of its Creator and brought to know God . . . Then put on the garments that suit God's chosen people, his own, his beloved: compassion, kindness, humility, gentleness, patience. Be forbearing with one another, and forgiving . . . you must forgive as the Lord forgave you. To crown all, there must be love, to bind all together and complete the whole. Let Christ's peace be arbiter in your hearts . . .' (Col. 2.10–15). The Christian experience is existential, in that commitment to Christ is something that alters the very basis of our existence – 'When anyone is united to Christ, there is a new world' (II Cor. 5.17). And it is that new world, of which we are now part, which we have with us as we make each moral decision. And, of course, each decision we make shapes us yet again. We create the world as we love, since we are re-creating ourselves and our impact upon it. Thus we have not just an ethic or a morality, but a life-style, a way of approaching the whole business of living.

It is the life-style that results directly from what God has done in becoming man. The moral responsibility has passed into man's hands, man is cut free from dependence on God, or written codes. Christianity in its life-style achieves the freedom which existentialism seeks – Sartre railing against God in his play *The Flies* is both a compelling critique of traditional religion and at the same time an uncanny description of the freedom made possible for man by an incarnate God:

You blundered – you should not have made me free . . . I *am* my freedom. No sooner had you created me than I ceased to be yours . . . Suddenly, out of the blue, freedom crashed down on me and swept me off my feet. Nature sprang back, my youth went with the wind, and I knew myself alone, utterly alone in the midst of this well-meaning little universe of yours. I was like a man who's lost his shadow. And there was nothing

left in heaven, no Right or Wrong, nor anyone to give me
orders ... I am doomed to have no other law but mine ...
In Nature are a thousand beaten paths all leading up to you –
but I must blaze my own trail. For I am a man, and every man
must find out his own way.[4]

The existentialist movement in France in this century has often
in its life-style touched very close to the spirit of what Christianity
was meant to be about, evidenced in the bold individualism of the
'chanson' – 'Nobody has the right to be / the judge of what is
right for me' (Charles Aznavour) – and in the exhilarating joy of
love and life that was celebrated in the French cinema, as, for
example, in the films of Claude Lelouch. As with the hippy
philosophy of the sixties, it would be foolish to claim an exact
parallel with the spirit of Christian love, but these do seem points
where secularism has come close to the heart of the thing, and so
serve well to illustrate something of what the Christian life-style
might achieve.

What, of course, also happens in such a life-style is that love
for God and love of neighbour merge into one. There will still
be endless dissertations till the end of time as to which comes
first, and which follows from which. But in truth the twin commands begin to complement each other, begin to become part of
the same experience, when both are lived out to the full. The
joyous 'high' cannot go on all the time – the disciples saw the
glory of Jesus on the mountain, and had to return to the plain –
but once you have seen what the place of love in life might be,
you will never be truly satisfied with anything else. In love for
each other, we do discover what life is meant to be, and we thus
discover love for God and God's love for us. And so the whole
becomes one life-style, one set of priorities, of ideals from which
we need never climb down. Love does, in truth, conquer all,
because it is the all-pervading force of the universe, which we are
privileged to glimpse every time we love or are loved. That was
always the way God was revealed. 'It is by this that we know
what love is: that Christ laid down his life for us ... Though God
has never been seen by any man, God himself dwells in us if we

love one another . . . God is love: he who dwells in love is dwelling in God, and God in him . . . If a man says "I love God" while hating his brother, he is a liar . . . he who loves God must also love his brother' (I John 3–4).

What we seek is a life-style that can celebrate love without fear because it is rooted and grounded in love itself. It will therefore bear all the marks of love – faith, repentance, spirituality, sensitivity and awareness, forgiveness, personal freedom and a true value of the self, the human soul. It will be the transcendence of man, the point at which man breaks through to Godhead just as God has broken through to him. It will make him truly man, utterly human, and thus mature, grown up into Christ. What he says, what he thinks, and even what he does will fall back into their proper place, and though these are the rungs by which he climbed up to make the breakthrough, it will be who he is that finally matters. It will be on the ethical and moral question of life-style by which mankind will finally be judged. As ever in the New Testament, it is the doing of the will of God, it is the loving that counts, however many pious exercises we go through. 'Not everyone who calls me "Lord, Lord" will enter the kingdom of Heaven, but only those who do the will of my heavenly Father' (Matt. 7.21). The test will be whether you and I are recognized by him – 'I never knew you' (Matt. 7.23). What we do to others, we do to him (25.40) and he will, as a result, recognize us. It was quite simply true that all you need is love, and when the other temporary realities have dissolved, and love is revealed as the only thing that ever really mattered, we shall need it more than ever. 'To love God is to keep his commands' (I John 5.3) and all his commands are to love.

FIVE

The Coming of the Kingdom

I sense through my experience that at the centre of creation and in the depths of my existence is the ultimate reality, which is love. To that reality I choose to give the name God. I believe that this love was concretely expressed and revealed in the human life and sacrificial death of Jesus of Nazareth, and that such love defeated death itself, so that Jesus may be regarded as alive, and so himself worshipped as God. As a result, the Spirit of God was unleashed on the world among men and women, enabling them to do two things. First, to draw near to and connect with love itself, and so find peace because they are in accord with the origin and purpose of life, and second, to live by the Spirit, loving in a 'situational' way without a book of rules, so that their love for one another may be genuine and effective. The Christian is thus led to an individual life-style whose purpose is peace and love – his life becomes about loving and being loved, and it is free to be so because the dividing line between mankind and the source of love, the God/man barrier, has been completely broken down.

The life of the individual Christian is one committed to love. Such a life-style leads him quite logically not just to a concern for another, but to a love of life itself. It is the ultimately positive response to life, and love, once grasped as the centre of things, and as an activity of which I am actually capable, makes the world a better place to live in. Life becomes not only worth living, but something worth building, improving. It is a very small step from learning to love another human being to having a concern for the whole quality of life. What the Christian faith does is place the highest possible value on human life (God is man), and the highest possible value on love (God is love). Once you have put such value on to those two concepts, you are committed not simply to loving other individuals, but to a vision of the world and the cosmos in which all is love, where human beings, without knowing one another, act towards one another by the principles that the faith has established. In other words, the Christian will soon find himself not only learning to love other individuals, but trying to play his part in establishing a context for love, a culture of love, an environment in which love can breed and grow. He needs to create an atmosphere in which others may catch such truth as he has found, from which others may put a similarly massive value on human beings and on love. The sensitivity and awareness needs to relate not simply to other human souls, but to the world in which souls are set. It needs to be a social awareness. As the God/man barrier is broken, mankind takes on the responsibility for loving and also the responsibility for the well-being, health, happiness, fulfilment and survival of his fellow human beings. If we meant what we said about God, if we meant what we said about mankind, if we meant what we said about love, then we are also in the game of society, of environment, of global issues, of mutual support and concern on a world-wide scale. It is an element of the faith which we fight hard to resist. We would, of course, much prefer religion to be, as they say, a personal matter, something between me and God, something about the way I treat individuals with whom I happen to come into contact. Charity begings at home. Once I open a can of beans about loving beyond that point, who knows what I might let out, or more strictly, let in to my life?

Michel Quoist expresses it perfectly in 'Why did you tell me to love?' He can cope with the first ones he is asked to love.

I welcomed them. I would have cared for them and fondled them . . .

Till then, it was sensible . . .

But he leaves the door of love open, and others start crowding in, people he does not know or care about, needing and demanding –

They come bending under heavy loads; loads of injustice, of resentment and hate, of suffering and sin . . .

They drag the world behind them, with everything rusted, twisted or badly adjusted.

Lord, they hurt me! They are in the way . . .[5]

We would like, by and large, to live our own Christian lives in our own way, and leave the problems of the world to others. But by putting such a value on human beings, all human beings, and having attached such importance to loving, that is the one thing we are not able to do. Thus almost every Christian finds himself or herself involved to some degree with, for want of a better phrase 'helping others', some charity, some concern outside the immediate, some cause, some people who are disadvantaged to the point where they cannot help themselves. Such help may be financial, it may be practical, it may be in terms of support. But I venture to suggest that it is a pretty odd sort of Christian whose vision does not extend somewhere beyond his own immediate concerns. A Christian who is not sensitive to and aware of the needs of a suffering society should examine very carefully whether he or she has really got hold of what the faith is about. The world we used to leave to God, now we wish to leave it to others. Christianity makes it our responsibility.

It is this culture, this atmosphere, this environment, this context, this vision of what the world and its society might be, that I understand to be what Jesus and the first Christians meant by 'the kingdom of God' or the 'kingdom of Heaven'. Just as the cross keeps before us what love should be, so the idea of the kingdom keeps ahead of us a vision of what we are working towards, a society, a domain, where love is made to work at all levels, where sensitivity, awareness, forgiveness, freedom pervade all levels of being, and all beings support one another. It is the idea which prevents us slipping back into the defeatism of 'Oh, well, that's human nature, and there is nothing we can do about it.' The whole thrust of Christianity is that there is everything that can be done about human nature, it can defeat death, it can be God. So a seemingly implacable world can be changed, the things we dream of can be achieved, because a society of love is envisaged in the scheme of things, a kingdom of God.

The New Testament treats the kingdom in two distinct ways, and in two distinct time-scales. In order to keep the vision high, we need to absorb them both. Arguably the first recorded words of Jesus are, 'The time has come: the kingdom of God is upon you' (Mark. 1.15). The kingdom is not to be seen as a dream of the future, but as something that is already here, that has already happened, that has already begun. 'The Pharisees asked him, "When will the kingdom of God come?" He said, "You cannot tell by observation when the kingdom of God comes. There will be no saying 'Look, here it is!' or 'there it is!': for in fact the kingdom of God is among you" ' (Luke 17.20–21). There is much discussion about how to translate that last phrase, and the New English Bible offers a variety of alternatives – 'the kingdom of God is *within* you', 'is within your grasp', 'will suddenly be among you'. But all imply the kingdom as begun and present. It is the massive upheaval of the relationship between God and man that ushers in this new state of affairs, that lays the groundwork and opens up the potential for such a society to become real. Such a society is already going on, already being built among those who love one another. When people begin to love in that sensitive, caring way that God has made possible for us, the kingdom is already sensed. We can see and feel among ourselves what we want for the world. We can sense the ingredients of which such a society will be made up. Similarly, the powers of Jesus himself were evidence that the kingdom had begun. 'If it is by the Spirit of God that I drive out the devils, then be sure the kingdom of God has already come upon you' (Matt. 12.28). Thus the effect of the Christ-event on an individual is to give him citizenship of the kingdom – 'He has brought us away into the kingdom of his dear Son' (Col. 1.13) – and to empower him not with a future hope but with the present realities that we saw to be the gifts and fruit of the Spirit: 'The kingdom of God is . . . justice, peace and joy, inspired by the Holy Spirit' (Rom. 14.17). The kingdom with all its signs and evidences was inaugurated by the life, death and resurrection of Christ. Once those events occurred. the outline shape of the will of God for the

world was drawn, and the shape is the kingdom, already existing
in the world and among us wherever love is allowed to surface,
and obscured where it is not.

While Jesus radically preached a present, already existing
kingdom of God, he also undeniably retained the Jewish notion
of a kingdom in the future, being built, being worked towards.
Thus he teaches his disciples to pray 'Your kingdom come'. He
tells stories about the kingdom as something that is to happen
after a time of growth and waiting. There is no doubt that there
is an apocalyptic strand in Jesus's teaching, and he almost certainly
envisaged the fulfilment of the kingdom in his own lifetime.
'There are some of those standing here who will not taste death
before they have seen the Son of Man coming in his kingdom'
(Matt. 16.28). It seems that Jesus was wrong. The apparently endless delay in such a hope must not preclude such an apocalyptic
conclusion to the world, but it nevertheless seems more likely that
what Jesus truly envisaged was the building of a society among
humanity that would reflect the love at the heart of things. Thus
as well as having begun, it is also in the process of being created,
it is the social task on which mankind is to be engaged if he is to be
truly man. As an individual, he is called to love; as a social animal,
he is called to bring into being the kingdom of God, a total society
governed by love.

So what, according to Jesus, is such a kingdom to be like? What
are the characteristics of this society to which we find ourselves
committed? The kingdom is entered through sacrifice; it may be
necessary to re-think old ties and relationships, it is created on the
ethical demands of God, and the risks that they involve. 'It is
better to enter the kingdom of God with one eye than to keep
both eyes and be thrown into hell' (Mark 9.47). The kingdom is
about being constantly awake and vigilant – 'you never know
the day or the hour' (Matt. 25). It is unlikely to be a home for the
self-righteous, but open rather to the unexpectedly broad vision
of God's love – 'Many will come from east and west to feast . . .
in the kingdom of heaven. But those who were born to the kingdom will be driven out into the dark' (Matt. 8.11–12) and it will
be hard 'for the wealthy to enter' (Mark 10.23). Many of Jesus's

stories begin with the words 'The kingdom is like this . . .' and each illustrates the sort of society to which we are working. Perhaps most important of all is Jesus's insistence that the kingdom will be entered with simplicity and humility:

> They brought children for him to touch. The disciples rebuked them, but when Jesus saw this, he was indignant, and said to them 'Let the children come to me; do not try to stop them; for the kingdom of God belongs to such as these. I tell you, whoever does not accept the kingdom of God like a child will never enter it.' And he put his arms round them, laid his hands upon them, and blessed them (Mark 10.13–16).

That is the spirit and the attitude that will shape and rule the kind of society to which Christians are committed. That is the hope we have for all our fellow-creatures. The kingdom that is already here, among us, functioning, will infect and infuse the world until we have created the kingdom for which we hope, visible in justice and peace. It is like mustard – 'as a seed . . . smaller than any other, but when it is grown, it is bigger than any garden-plant' (Matt. 13.31). It is like yeast 'which a woman took and mixed . . . with flour till it was all leavened' (13.33). It is like 'treasure lying buried in a field' (13.44) or a beautiful pearl of incredible value which somebody 'sold everything he had and bought' (13.46). Imperceptibly, but irresistibly, the kingdom is taking shape – men and women of vision through the centuries are led to put new pieces into the jigsaw, to bring the reality a step nearer. Those who try to construct any other kind of society will in the final analysis find themselves in the wrong place.

We must not under-estimate the centrality of the idea of the kingdom. There was a day when particularly those in the caring professions found it fashionable to speak of 'purposes, aims and objectives'. A purpose was the short-term intention for today, tomorrow, this week; an aim was the reason you were involved in the exercise, which you might expect to see fulfilled in a year, five years, ten years; your objective was your ultimate reason, the thing you were finally after, the force that drives you, the vision to be held ahead of you, which you may never hope to see in its entirety. The kingdom is every Christian's objective. In the process of decision-making, it is the final test by which all things are measured. It is the first priority on our time and money. Too many Christians seem to be under the impression that if they are saying the right religious things, having the appropriate emotional sensations, going through the acceptable rituals, then no more is required of them. It is not true. Their top priority is the building of the kingdom. It is not an optional extra, a peripheral Christian matter for those who like to get involved in social concerns. It is of the essence of Christianity. I understand your worries, says Jesus, I know you have to think about what to eat, what to wear, how to pay the mortgage, whether the church roof will stay on, what form the liturgy should take, whether you're reading the Bible enough – but just 'set your mind on God's kingdom and his justice before everything else, and all the rest will come to you as well,' everything else will fall into perspective. The kingdom and justice before everything else – that is part of the existential life-style. 'Do not be anxious about tomorrow; tomorrow will look after itself' (Matt. 6.33–34). I would like that passage read at the start of every board meeting, every business meeting, including church councils and committees. Perhaps when the kingdom is fulfilled, it will be.

The Christian is committed to love of God and love of his neighbour. That entails him in a personal faith and spirituality, and in a life-style where love controls his personal relationships. But it also entails him in playing a part in constructing a society which reflects the love of God and the glory of mankind. It will be a society based on the self-same principles of love that we explored in personal relationships. Now we must write them large. We must create a world in which everyone is sensitive to the needs of others, where we are aware of each other; a world where forgiveness and the possibility of a fresh start replace our natural inclination to seek revenge, where people's needs are met because their needs exist, not because they deserve help or have earned the right to charity; a world where every individual is allowed his personal freedom, and where others remove, by force if necessary, the man-made constraints that prevent him from having such freedom. All that we claimed for our own lives through Christ, all that we said we sought to give to others, we must now contribute to the whole. This, of course, opens up a thousand issues, and there is no way that any one individual can be realistically involved in all of them. One must presumably settle one's talents and enthusiasm somewhere, wherever needs are there to be met; whether, to be specific, among those who are homeless or only have inadequate housing, among the depressed and suicidal, who feel unloved, among children in need, or the aged, or the handicapped, physically or mentally, among those in prison for what they believe rather than for any crime they have committed, among the animal welfare movement, or pressure groups in the environment. In all these areas, and all the others one cares to raise, there are channels for caring: Shelter, the Samaritans, the children's societies and homes, Help the Aged, Mind, Amnesty International, Green Peace, Friends of the Earth, and many, many more. Christians are involved in all of them at every level, many were begun with the inspiration of Christians committed to the kingdom. However countless the needs, the issues and the channels, and however few of them any individual can enter, what is important is that the Christian faith is manifestly seen to have this dimension. Too often, Christians have appeared to duck the real needs, the real issues of the world they live in, in favour of more 'religious', more 'spiritual' concerns. Whereas in truth, there is no activity more religious, more spiritual, more acceptable to God than the meeting of human need.

In these simple ways, by simple support with a cheque-book, or a few hours of time, or by summoning up sheer human concern, the kingdom is created, and mountains moved. But we live in a complex world. There are points as individuals that become sticking points. Some needs grow faster than we are able to meet them. In many areas, and to some extent, in all of them, we need, in order to build the kingdom, more than a growing number of willing hands. We need to change more fundamentally the priorities of those around us. Some of that we may do by persistent example, but still there will come the feeling of knocking one's head against brick walls. The channels of involvement can take us so far, and we may often satisfy our own need to offer love. But the true needs of others are not always met, since the odds are too heavily stacked against them. And suddenly, it is more than love that they need, or rather, it is love in a specific form, it is a love that will shift the ground on which they stand, it is love that will discriminate in the favour of those in need, it is love that will demand from the rest of the world a re-assessment of its values and priorities. It is the cry for justice. 'In problems concerning corporate groups', wrote Archbishop Temple, 'the way of love lies through justice.'

And as a word like 'justice' enters the argument, we have found that Christian faith is, whether we like it or not, about politics, and that politics are not peripheral, either, but essential to the creation of the kingdom, which is political or else it is a fantasy.

Let us clear out of the way first the age-old claim that religion should keep out of politics, and that the two should not be allowed to mix, because if that is true, Christian faith and practice have reached a dead end, come to the end of their power and effectiveness. Firstly, it is not a claim that the Bible would share at any point. The Old Testament as a whole is a record of God's dealings with a nation in history. The religious decisions are the political ones, like whether or not there should be a king, or who should attack whom, where and when. And the prophets are, without exception, massive political agitators. The whole spiritual health of the nation is assessed by its political life, what matters to God is treatment of poverty, the laziness of the rich, corruption in the forces of law and order, dishonesty in trade. Over and over again, they ask the political questions: 'Is not this what I require of you . . . to loose the fetters of injustice . . . to set free those who have been crushed?' (Isa. 58.6). Amos, above all, savages a society of idle rich: 'I will break down both winter-house and summer-house; houses of ivory shall perish, and great houses be demolished . . . Hate evil and love good, enthrone justice in the courts . . . I cannot endure the music of your lutes. Let justice roll on like a river . . . You who loll on beds inlaid with ivory, and sprawl

over your couches ... you have turned into venom the process
of law, and justice itself into poison.' On the contrary, pleads
Zechariah, 'administer true justice, show loyalty and compassion
to one another, do not oppress the orphan and the widow, the
alien and the poor' (Zech. 7.9–10). And these are political issues,
and they are political because they are issues that cannot be
avoided.

Religion and politics are totally bound up with each other
because their area of concern is a complete overlap. Both are
concerned with the whole of life, the whole of mankind's experience. There is no political issue that does not have profound
religious and spiritual implications, and there is no religious belief
that does not have direct political effects. Inter-action between the
two is totally unavoidable unless you stunt or limit either or both
to the point where they have no meaning at all. Men and women
are political animals, they are part of an ordered society, they
have a place and rights within it, they increasingly demand the
powers to change its ordering should they see fit. They cannot be
non-political unless they are cast away alone on a desert island,
or dead. They may choose not to comment on or exercise their
political nature, to opt out of responsibility in this regard, but
that is a profoundly political thing to do, and of a highly destruc-
tive kind. Similarly, men and women are religious animals, the
spirit is let loose within them, and the kingdom of God growing
among them. Every political decision made, any decision about
the ordering of life, at whatever level, echoes into eternity as a
vindication of or as violence to the ultimate law of love. Every
political decision made affects a human being somewhere, and it
enhances or destroys love within him, it builds or prevents the
kingdom of God. To deny that this is so is its own madness, its
own destructiveness. Those who claim to be Christians and who
pretend to 'keep out of politics' are making the most profound
political statement of all, namely that everything is all right as it
is, and needs no comment. Saying nothing means something. A
minister, for example, who survived the Vietnam war without
mentioning it from the pulpit, was for its duration, proclaiming
loudly and clearly his approval of it. A letter to a newspaper

recently asked why more churches were not giving money and food to the miners' strike fund. A church member replied that to do so would be to take a political stance. A third correspondent pointed out that *not* to send money and food to the miners' strike fund was also a political stance. Anyone who believes that religion *can* keep out of politics is living in an illogical fools' paradise.

And, let us not fool ourselves, when people say 'religion should keep out of politics', they are not criticising the minister who by silence expressed his support for Vietnam, or the church who expressed its support for the National Coal Board by not sending relief to the miners. Politics that supports the *status quo* is perfectly acceptable from Christians – it is only those who wish to change things who should 'keep out'. What they really mean is 'Christians who are left-wing should keep out of politics.' Which is rather a different thing.

A fundamental question for Christians in this regard will obviously be: Was Jesus himself a political figure? The answer, of course, is yes, he was, because he was a human being. What people more usually mean by the question is whether or not he was a member of the Zealot party, which was committed to throwing off the yoke of Rome. To which the answer is probably no, although we do know that one of his close disciples was a Zealot. There is also little doubt that part of the crushing disappointment at his death resulted from his apparent failure to rid Israel of its foreign domination. One theory proposes that Judas Iscariot betrayed Jesus so that he would be forced into political action against Rome. Luke records that the disciples were still asking the question after the resurrection. 'When they were all together, they asked him "Lord, is this the time when you are to establish once again the sovereignty of Israel?" ' (Acts 1.6). Thus at least part of the hope placed in him was of an immediate political kind. Jesus, by and large, seems to refuse to be drawn into too limiting a political position. Though that does not mean, as the 'religion should keep out of politics' brigade would have us believe, that he ducked out of the political questions altogether. Most of the parables have direct political implications. But it is usual to throw in our faces the famous quotation, 'Pay Caesar what is due to Caesar, and pay God what is due to God' (Matt. 22.17). This is usually interpreted as a clever and ambivolent answer to the question about whether taxes should be paid, and that the answer is yes, you should pay taxes, on the grounds that political leaders should get on with their job while the religious get on with theirs. In other words, religion should keep out of politics. But it must be acknowledged that this is a massive piece of interpretation, a gloss on the original story. In *Unyoung, Uncoloured, Unpoor*,[6] Colin Morris pointed out two things about the story. First, that when asked about paying taxes, Jesus has to ask his questioners for a Roman coin. Why was he not carrying such a coin himself? In fact, there were Jews who refused to carry the money of the occupying power – they were the Zealots and their sympathizers. And second, the question Jesus is asked is not about taxes in general, but about taxes to be paid by an occupied people to the occupying power. He is saying to people who despise Caesar and everything he stands for, 'Pay Cesar what is due to Caesar.' It was like saying, 'Give Hitler what you think he deserves' to the French Resistance, or 'Give the Kremlin what you think it is worth' to Hungarians during the uprising. Nothing can be proved, but what Morris does illustrate convincingly is that the saying may equally well be interpreted as a highly inflammatory statement. The political stance of Jesus is a great deal more ambiguous that we are often led to believe, and since little was written down for a generation, it is quite likely that there are many immediately topical sayings that have been lost anyway.

And the sum total of all that is that Christians are involved in politics by virtue of their humanity, and need not be ashamed of being so, or pressured out of being so. Thus I go on to mention three further issues of the kingdom which take us whether we like it or not into the political arena. We do not enter that arena because we wish to be political, let alone deliberately provocative, but because our vision of the kingdom of love takes us there. These are the three big ones, these, it seems to me, are the three issues that no Christian can avoid, and therefore every Christian is obliged to be involved in. They are also the three issues that are simply too big to be approached on an individual basis, and they therefore demand to be taken up as causes, and involve us in direct political pressure. But we are driven there not for effect, but out of love. All three arise for us because we are sensitive and aware of other people in our world, because we are committed to forgiveness and the meeting of needs, and because we believe that each individual has the right to the freedom to be himself. They arise because absolutely intrinsic to the kingdom are three things which have no place.

The first of these is hunger. In the kingdom, food is shared and all have enough to eat. No mother watches her child die of starvation. In the world we live in, there is more than enough for everyone, but the fat rich deliberately withhold food from over half the world. There is no need to rehearse the arguments; everyone now knows what is going on, the television pictures have to reach a level of unbearable gruesomeness before anyone takes any notice. The conscience of the West was massively stirred by the sights of Ethiopia in 1984. The charity organizations tell us that they foresaw the famine two years earlier, that they informed the Western governments, that the British government, and our representatives in the European parliament deliberately voted against an aid programme for Ethiopia because they disliked the country's politics. In 1984, the British government proposed a massive cut in overseas aid. And these are the people who tell us religion should keep out of politics. Of course they will tell us that, because the kingdom of God would expose the greed, selfishness, hypocrisy of their position. Poverty is allowed to go on, half the world is allowed to starve to death, so that we may retain a farcically high standard of living, so that power may reside where it is, and the order not be changed. The kingdom demands that the order must be changed. Half the world starving to death is absolutely unacceptable. The facts and the moral arguments have stared us in the face now for two decades, and the Brandt Commission exposed the dangers very clearly. The excuses made by the rich nations are now wearing very thin. There is quite simply enough food to go round and it must be released. It is quite absurd that the issues of the so-called 'third' world (there is only one world) should be left to charities and to individuals. It is time that those in power in the rich nations faced up to their responsibilities. Apart from the sheer callousness with which they watch their fellow human beings die, their thinking is absurdly short-term. If they do not do something soon, one or both of two things will happen, if they have not already begun. First, the nations who are forced to watch their people die will realize that they are going to have to demand their share of the world's cake. They will arm, they will stir up the political will and they will demand. We must not assume that because people are starving that they are necessarily stupid. They are coming to realize their rights as human beings, and the selfishness of the rich could yet unleash on the world a conflict rooted in so much anger that no one will survive. And second, it is now twenty years since I heard a Christian economist prophesy that if we failed to feed the other half of the world, we would eventually all starve to death. And we already see poverty, hunger, unemployment has come home to us. The same selfish attitudes prevail. Along with a 'third' world, we are coming to accept what Bishop David Sheppard calls 'the other Britain'. We are dangerously close, just as we use the 'third' world to bolster our own power and trade, to using the poor, to allowing them to exist, in order to maintain the status quo, in order to retain power where it is. We are again shoring ourselves up against bitter conflict. The kingdom of God is a place where nobody starves, where poverty does not exist. We are called to create that kingdom. Granted the resistance and the vested interests which will refuse to yield, which will turn very nasty if they had to do so to save the life of one pathetic empty-bellied aching African child, Christians have to realize that they are up against something almost too selfish and too vicious to contemplate. But the sharing of the world's resources is an absolute priority if our objective is the kingdom, and Christians will not let a single chance to press it go by.

The second thing which has no place in the kingdom is war and the fear of war. It is quite simply immoral and inhuman that the world is required to live with the threat of annihilation from weapons of the destructiveness of the nuclear arsenals. There is no interpretation of the Christian faith or the kingdom of God that can allow the nuclear arms race to continue. Christians will by definition be committed to the establishing of peace, and in the context of this world, that means to the dismantling and abolition of all nuclear weapons. There are some who claim that they may be morally preserved as a deterrent. The argument is a nonsense, and has been exploded by both right and left of the political spectrum – if you claim that your nuclear weapons are to deter, then they are not intended for use, and if they are not intended for use, they are a lousy deterrent. There are others who are prepared to gamble with human lives by holding on to these weapons until everyone has agreed to get rid of them. They say they wish to disarm 'multi-laterally'. They have been saying that for thirty years, and they have not disarmed anything. Indeed under their guidance, nuclear weapons have proliferated to a terrifying degree. Sheer commonsense tells us that if they go on multiplying, sooner or later, they will get into the wrong hands, or some idiot will press the button, or a human or technical error will set one off, and we have actually destroyed all life for ever on this planet. And, let us make no mistake, the suggestion that we shall be emerging from cupboards after a fortnight, wiping the radioactive dust from our cups and making tea is a cruel illusion and a confidence trick perpetrated by people who do not wish to relinquish power. Once again, the arguments have been rehearsed so often, they are well known. It is just that Christians will be in the forefront of those who take them seriously. If we intend to create the kingdom, we are obliged to be part of the peace movement, which, to be blunt, means, in this country, the Campaign for Nuclear Disarmament. There is no denying that unilateral disarmament also carries its risks, though risks are built in to Christian living, and the risks here are not as horrendous or irresponsible as those of proliferation. There is some truth in the banner which reads 'A unilateralist is a multilateralist who means it.'

But the simplest and most profound argument of all is that we do not, if we put any value on human life at all, have the right to insist that our fellow human beings, that our children, should live in a state of fear. Like hunger, such fear could well provoke a state of social unrest that we can hardly imagine, if it is not already doing so.

Towards the end of the last Labour administration, somewhere around 1978, the following letter appeared in *The Guardian*. I reproduce it in full:

Sir – In a full-scale exchange of nuclear warheads you would probably die. So would two-thirds of your family and friends. Some of us would die very quickly, others more slowly and terribly, in hours, weeks or years. If we survived, we could never be sure that children born to us would be whole and healthy. Our cities would be ruined, our country devastated and our culture lost; and we would be governed, from underground, by cowards who refused to stay and face the consequences of their actions.

Who are they, these governors of the charred and mutilated, these counters of the dead? Why do they live buried underneath the earth while we on the surface die? We should know the names, surely, of those we are dying for. Margaret Thatcher, James Callaghan, Francis Pym, William Rodgers. One woman and three men with the power to kill 35 million people or more who live in this land. One woman and three men who build caverns for themselves and their fellow-governors and leave us, the people of this country, to die on the surface and witness its devastation. Cowards, all four. Why should we die for them?

It is a horror to think of, the death of people we love, and the ruin of places we know. But we must think of it because if we do not, it will happen. The leaders of our two main political parties and their defence secretaries have got together and planned it.

They know how we will die. It is written down in little Home Office pamphlets, which we mustn't see because they are frightening. I have seen them and I am frightened. I am frightened for my life and the lives of those I love. I do not trust these four people with their little private burrows and their red buttons. They will kill us unless we stop them.

And we can stop them. They live in London, these four, and they work in the Houses of Parliament. We must go to them and tell them that we do not want nuclear bombs in this country, anywhere. We must give our support to those others in parliament who have promised to remove the bombs. We must go to London, all those of us who want to go on living and tell them to their faces that if they don't get rid of nuclear bombs we will get rid of them. It is we who will die, not them. And we do not want to die.

Yours sincerely,

It is out-of-date now, of course, but it remains very powerful, because it is simple and it tells the truth. It points up who are the realists and who the muddle-headed idealists. They may try to lead us into Cloud Cuckoo Land: we, on the other hand, are constructing the kingdom of God. And somewhere deep down, by the standards of the kingdom, there is something seriously wrong with a society in which, for example, the smoking of cannabis is illegal, and the manufacture of nuclear weapons is not.

The third of the great kingdom issues is the stereo-typing of human beings as a result of their racial characteristics. It is deep-rooted in man's fear of the stranger, of the unknown; and racism surfaces, like poverty and war, wherever those in power are afraid of losing it. A race of people becomes a scapegoat. It is bad enough to regard people as inferior because of their opinions or their class or their intelligence, but to do so on grounds of race or sex is both vicious and cowardly. The two societies in this century which have least resembled the kingdom are without doubt Germany under Hitler and present-day South Africa, which have racial hatred in common. It beds down very easily though in all societies that are discontented, it is the easy route to violence, and it is no coincidence that the city riots in Britain in 1981 had a racial element, nor that a turning point in the 1979 election campaign was Mrs Thatcher's famous statement about the fear of being 'swamped' by immigrants. No amount of exhortation will rid most parts of the world of racism now – creating the kingdom will mean support for a persistent combination of anti-discrimination law firmly and ruthlessly applied together with a sturdy growth of a dedicated public opinion. If there is one area where we must increase the sense of guilt, it is here; the racist must be made to feel ostracized. If society is able to make, for example, the smoking of tobacco appear anti-social, it can do the same for the more serious evil of racism, and the sick groups that advocate it must simply not be allowed to thrive. Evil must be seen for what it is. We do no service to the kingdom by condoning or excusing it. It is therefore kingdom-work to isolate racist countries and racist elements in our own.

Let me repeat, the Christian enters into these three areas, not for the sake of political involvement *per se*, but because these are three fundamental breaches of the law of love to which Christianity is committed. Out of love for fellow human beings, Christians are obliged to be involved to some degree in all three, whatever other charities or causes they support. I do not understand a Christian who does not feel so obliged. And it so happens that the building of the kingdom is in all three cases common sense as well as love. In all cases, too, money and power are key factors in the wish of others to preserve things as they are, so in defining the kingdom, we will need to understand quite clearly the Christian attitude to both of these.

First, power and authority. Jesus made the position quite clear – all earthly authority is derived from him, it is not a human virtue. 'Full authority in heaven and on earth has been committed to me' (Matt. 28.18). Jesus's own authority derives from his ability and willingness to serve others. 'You know that in the world, the recognized rulers lord it over their subjects, and their great men make them feel the weight of authority. That is not the way with you: among you, whoever wants to be great must be your servant, and whoever wants to be first must be the willing slave of all. For even the Son of Man did not come to be served but to serve, and to give up his life as a ransom for many' (Mark 10.42–45). That is the last word on authority. Perhaps the most moving story in the New Testament, even more moving than the story of the crucifixion, is the account in John's Gospel of Jesus washing the feet of his disciples (John 13). It came as a shock to them, displaying the Christian concept of authority in a peculiarly vivid way. It illustrates a pattern of mutual service which does not come naturally to man. Power only resides in those who serve others, who set about the meeting of needs. Those who refuse to do so abrogate their power, and can claim no authority. That is why, although Paul argues that in general Christians should be concerned for civil obedience, he nevertheless allows for the possibility that those in authority will sometimes ask for more than their rights: 'Pay every government official what he has a right to ask' (Rom. 13.7 – Jerusalem Bible). And so in the end the kingdom belongs to those who enter it like children – 'those who know their need of God', the sorrowful, the gentle, 'those who hunger and thirst to see right prevail ... those who show mercy ... those whose hearts are pure, the peacemakers' (Matt. 5.3–10). It is they who have real authority.

The New Testament is equally clear on the Christian attitude to money. It is a rival god. 'No servant can be the slave of two masters ... You cannot serve God and money' (Matt. 6.24). The accumulation of money, 'the creation of wealth' as it is fashionably called, is expressly forbidden. 'Do not store up for yourselves treasure on earth ... Where your treasure is, there will your heart be also (6.19, 21). Paul goes further: 'The love of money is the root of all evil things' (I Tim. 6.10). It would be very comforting for all of us if God would be even slightly ambiguous in the matter. But he is not. Money is not the source or goal of anything. 'You, man of God, must shun all this, and pursue justice, piety, fidelity, love, fortitude and gentleness' (6.11). Perhaps the saddest story in the New Testament is that of the young man who comes to Jesus willing to obey the basic commands of God, indeed he claims to have done so since his childhood. But he is trapped by his own wealth and possessions, and when Jesus tells him that discipleship will mean parting with them, he can only go away heavy-hearted (Matt. 19.16–22). Christians who find the accumulation of wealth compatible with their faith need again to hear the voice of Jesus. 'A rich man will find it hard to enter the kingdom of heaven. I repeat, it is easier for a camel to pass through the eye of a needle than for a rich man to enter the kingdom of God' (19.23). Attempts are often made to temper that saying by explaining that Jesus did not mean us to take it literally. Such attempts are usually made by Christians who are rather well-off.

It is partly because Christianity's attitude to power and to money are so uncompromising and strident that in some societies, it becomes a positively divisive force. Where money and power are the rulers, the kingdom will take shape only by upheaval, by a quite conscious reversal of the values of the world. It is natural, understandable, even forgiveable for human beings to slide into a system where power and money must hold sway, and from that breeding ground in particular will come the slime of racism, poverty and the threat of war. These become necessary to keep power and money in place. The kingdom will not then co-exist with secular society, and secular society will use everything in its power to distort, abuse and seek to destroy the claims of the kingdom. 'Ever since the coming of John the Baptist, the kingdom of heaven has been subjected to violence, and violent men are seizing it' (Matt. 11.12). Thus, too, a whole strand of Jesus's 'kingdom' stories and with a division of the wheat from the chaff (Matt. 13.36–43), of the good fish from the bad (13.47–50), of the forgiving from the unforgiving (18.23–35), of those who come to the feast from those who refuse (22.1–10), of the loving from the unloving (25.31–46). Christianity, as it creates the kingdom's values within society, will inevitably be required to sift and divide the values that society already holds. In that process, Christianity will not always be the paperer-over of cracks, it will sometimes be required to take sides, and most especially in those societies where power or money or both have been allowed to take control.

Thus, Christians will have a particular task, a particular upheaval to make, in societies where power is being abused, or where it is held by a small elite who refuse to have power wrested from them except by violence and from within their own ranks. These are the totalitarian societies, best represented today by the so-called communist countries of the Eastern block. The Christian kingdom of sensitivity, forgiveness and freedom can only grow in opposition to such a system, and will be expressed most clearly when in confrontation with those in power. The most glaring example of this has been the identification of Christians with the Solidarity movement in Poland, where the rights and freedoms of human beings are at stake. Those who hold power may crush such movements of the Spirit for a time, but the kingdom must finally emerge because the law of love is paramount. And it may be that the role of Christianity in such a context is to divide, to break through with a kind of violence to establish a pattern of mutual concern and service and to establish the right of every individual to freedom of expression and association.

What it is harder and more painful for us to recognize is that Christianity is equally opposed to a system where money is the controlling factor, and power allowed to rest with those who deal in it. In short, that capitalism in its raw state is as obnoxious to Christianity as totalitarianism. Its philosophy is precisely opposite to the teaching of Jesus on money, and it is willing to sacrifice people for the sake of financial gain. It thrives on the myth that financial gain will in the long term benefit people without any evidence that it does so. It is prepared to allow poverty and unemployment on a wide scale, it will trade with racist regimes, it will permit the proliferation of nuclear weapons in the name of its gods of growth and profit. It is the real 'permissive' society in that anything is permitted if it makes a profit, hence, for example, the spread of 'video nasties' in such societies. If there is a demand, and money can be made, they are justified. The system encourages competition, so that there will be winners and losers, and lame ducks go to the wall. They call it 'creating wealth' – in fact, it is the accumulation of profit for some at the expense of others. It is inconceivable that, for example, a Christian lawyer should in Russia be prepared to interrogate and torture dissidents. It is equally inconceivable that, say, a Christian dentist in this country should be part of a practice restricted to private patients; he is colluding with a corrupt system to make himself richer at the expense of those who cannot afford his services. Any system in which the rich grow richer and the poor poorer is repugnant to the kingdom.

In current Western society, the clear distinction between the opposite philosophies of capitalism and Christianity is evidenced in the manifestly low priority placed by the system on the meeting of needs. The earliest sacrifices in such a regime are education, health care, social services. These do not make money, they only meet needs, and so people must ultimately finance them for themselves. There is no community responsibility for people, only for profit. The people and their communities may be justifiably sacrificed, in the cause of economic growth. For the Christian, of course, such a philosophy is untenable and intolerable. It makes a god of money, and creates a divided society directly opposed to the kingdom. Some years back, Bishop Stockwood caused a stir with his statement that it was impossible to be a Christian and a Conservative. That cannot be quite true, since there are those who seem able to claim to be both. What I think may be said is that such people have either not understood the true nature of the capitalist system, or that they have not grasped the fundamentals of Christian faith.

When either system, whether based on power or money, is threatened, it tends to panic, and it shows its fear in repressive measures. The Eastern bloc has come to a point where such measures are taken continually, and Russia has been prepared to invade and crush its neighbour states if it senses any threat to its power. The reactions of a capitalist state are basically the same, though carried out with rather more subtlety. In the last few years in Britain, we have seen events which would have shocked a generation ahead of us. The government arbitrarily ban membership of a trade union at GCHQ, and offer bribes for people to relinquish their union rights. They claim it is on grounds of 'national security', and I imagine the Polish leaders say much the same. A young civil servant was gaoled like a common criminal because she told a newspaper about a letter from one democratically elected leader to another about a missile which could destroy this country, and which we who elected them and we who stand to be eliminated were not supposed to see. In a civilized country, such public spirit would be honoured. Most recently, at the time of writing, there is an intention to over-ride democratic decisions in our major cities, cancel elections and replace elected bodies with state appointees. One wonders whether such a step would have been taken if the cities were not being successfully run by parties opposed to the government. One fears what the government will do if opinion polls were to suggest that they might lose a General Election.

Most worrying of all, in any of these states, is the level of violence that is found to be acceptable to keep things as they are. Of course, violence in a sense is going on all the time; the lame ducks, the poor, the sick, the unemployed are all victims of violence by the state. Old people literally die of cold during our winters because there is not enough money to care for them, although money miraculously appears to pay for foreign nuclear missiles on our soil, or for us to fight a war in the South Atlantic. We should not be prepared to live with such violence. But we are more fearful still when the state begins to make use of the police and the armed forces for political purposes. It was where Hitler's Gestapo ended up, it is what the Russian secret police are about. The movement of police around Britain, being drafted away from their areas of work, and the way in which they are being asked to defend one set of people and not others, is a very worrying development. During the 1984 miners' strike, they were specifically helping working miners to exercise their right to work, but not helping striking miners to picket. As the police become less and less accountable, we know less and less about their aims, priorities, activities. The phrase 'death in police custody' is beginning to carry sinister overtones.

As far back as 1969, in his powerful and prophetic little book *Soul on Ice*, Eldridge Cleaver foresaw what Western society was becoming in this respect: 'The police department and the armed forces are the two arms of the power structure ... They have deadly weapons with which to inflict pain on the human body ... They use force, to make you do what the deciders have decided you must do ... The police do on the domestic level what the armed forces do on the international level: protect the way of life of those in power ... They follow orders. Orders flow from the top down.'[7] Cleaver's words remain an awful warning.

Totalitarianism and capitalism are the easy natural states into which human beings will slide without any sense of love and justice. They must be set in direct contrast to the kingdom of God. But it would be foolish to identify the kingdom with any one other political strand, or make it co-terminus with any political party. Clearly, Christianity will be best expressed through some kind of democratic socialism, though that term is so broad that it does allow for considerable variation. It will not, let us be clear, bear any relation to what the Soviet Union thinks of as socialism. If that is socialism, it is an abuse of it, and socialists should not be judged by it any more than Christians would wish to be judged by the Spanish Inquisition. Any talk of socialists having 'friends in Moscow' any more than, say, friends in Paris, is nonsense. Nor does socialism necessarily have to be limited to the teachings of Marx. Socialism was around for a long time before Marx, and Tony Benn, for example, in his *Arguments for Democracy* says that his 'political commitment owes much more to the teachings of Jesus ... than to the writings of Marx whose analysis seems to lack an understanding of the deeper needs of humanity.'[8] And that is, in point of fact, the crunch. Christianity is not to be identified with socialism or vice versa, but socialism does share with Christianity, in fact, let us not be falsely modest, has drawn from Christianity, a sense of the value of human beings and their dignity and an ethical priority of love and justice. It therefore shares at least part of the same social vision as Christianity, though it may not accept the same reasons for it. The nub of the matter is that socialism of a democratic kind is the only political philosophy we have based on the concept of the brotherhood of man. Whether atheists like it or not, that concept flows from the idea of the Fatherhood of God. What we in fact sensed back there was that God was loving us, what the kingdom reveals to us is that God the Father is loving all men and women equally. We can glibly say it. But it means that the child in Ethiopia, the unemployed man in Liverpool, the black youth in Bristol and so on and so on are my brothers and sisters, that they have a right to

my love and compassion and to food, and to work, and to equal
rights. Again, we may glibly say it, teach our children to sing
about it, but democratic socialism is the only political philosophy
that takes it as a premise. It is no good beginning somewhere else
and tinkering, trying to hint at socialist compassion to a totalitarian or capitalist base. It is the premise that counts.

There will be those who feel we have come a long way from the
basic Christian faith. I would dispute that. We are not on the
periphary. We are still at the centre, in that the Fatherhood of
God and therefore the brotherhood and sisterhood of mankind
are, as they used to say, of the esse of the faith. The faith simply
does not exist if it is not also put into practice at an individual level
with love and at a communal level with some form of socialism.
Christianity becomes far too easily an escape route – into the
starry heavens, into the Holy Land of two thousand years ago,
into mystical experience. We can even fool ourselves into thinking that if we mention God enough, if our natural home feels like
the shores of Galilee, if we can close our eyes and have warm
thoughts of heaven, that we are automatically loving other people
at the same time. But the question of political commitment brings
the thing right down to earth. People are dying right here – of
hunger, of torture, of war, of poverty, of violence, of racism, of
fear, of sadness. And the simple question is posed, 'What are you
going to do about it?' The time is long since past when we could
get away with shrugging our shoulders and saying that there is
nothing we can do. We have to break the habit, ours and others,
of watching television and saying 'How terrible'. Christianity is
about entering the world, loving it and saving it. That is what
Jesus did. That was his mission, and it is our mission. The building of the kingdom of God by the political involvement of
Christians in mission, witness and evangelism. We are not finally
interested in persuading people to enter mystical, wafer-thin
worlds of services in dark churches, nor in whipping up a frenzy
about Bible texts. We do not want more members for the club,
or if we do, only if they will turn right back into the world again,
as Jesus did, and feed it with the love they have found. If you
call yourself Christian, and you are not involved in loving at this

point, if you are not building the kingdom in this sense, then it was not love you found in the universe, but an extension of yourself, and what you call faith is just a cosmic ego-trip.

Day by day, we pray 'Your kingdom come, your will be done on earth as it is in heaven.' Sooner or later, we have to decide whether we want that prayer answered or not. If we do, then our commitment to God and to love will also entail our commitment to the elimination of hunger and poverty, of war and the fear of war, of racism and violence, of all that prevents human beings from loving and being loved. That means a commitment to the brotherhood and sisterhood of mankind and to the politics that flow from it. What we have to prove to the world is that what they call 'ideals' – love, peace, justice, sharing, compassion – are the only true realties, that the kingdom of God is made up of these things. The only way we can prove it is by constructing such a society here and now. The kingdom has, in point of fact, arrived and begun, it is moving among us. We have to tap it, pull it to the surface. We have to latch on to and build from the songs of love, the calls to peace, the non-violent action, till we have helped others to sense the atmosphere of what life might be like. It may go on in back rooms, on cold nights around the cruise missile sites, in trucks driving to Africa with grain, around camp fires, in the struggle for equality in the black townships, in memories of Ghandi, Martin Luther King, John Lennon. The kingdom has come, and the kingdom is now. We are called against all the odds, if necessary, to build the culture that will expose it.

SIX

Together

From this point on, it seems to me, it is primarily a matter of
'how'. We know, up to a point, what we are able to believe – we
now search for the ability to relate to the love that we have found
in such a way to bring us peace of mind and integrity of action.
We need to deepen our own relationship with the Christ of faith
so that our lives may more genuinely reflect the life of Jesus. We
need to find ways in which we ourselves become the channels by
which the Holy Spirit is let loose among us. We also know, up
to a point, what we are after to achieve these ends. We need to
learn how to love, how to make each personal relationship we
have part of a life-style of love and peace. We need to work out
how our progress towards the kingdom can be made effective in
the here and now, how we actually build the culture of politics
and society that the Kingdom requires. There will be several
answers to the question 'how', but there is one that the early
Christians found almost without thinking, and which simple
logic drives us to very quickly. If Christianity is about loving and
being loved, the one thing it cannot be is a philosophy for isolated individuals. My views on love can be genuine, accurate and
wholly praiseworthy as long as I sit alone in my room – it is when
someone else comes in, or when I am out with others, that the
problems of loving begin. If it is to be made to work, it is something that people will be doing together.

The first Christians functioned as a group, as a kind of extended
family, from a very early point. Almost from the moment that
Jesus began to gather the first disciples around him, it was clear
that human beings functioning together was to be at the core of

what he intended to demonstrate. The band of fishermen and others who stayed with him must have created as much effect as anything that Jesus himself said and did. The culture into which he came had, of course, a peculiar sense already of being one nation, one people under one God, so the concept of community living and experience should not have been totally alien. Though presumably this kind did not fit in with respectable norms. Thus, it becomes almost natural that after Jesus's death, and after the communal experience of his resurrection, the group should stick together. It comes as no surprise to find that 'late that Sunday evening, the disciples were together behind locked doors for fear of the Jews' (John 20.19), that in the following weeks 'they went to the room upstairs where they were lodging . . . constantly at prayer together' (Acts 1.13–14) and that by Pentecost, they were still 'all together in one place' (2.1). They had become not just the first Christians, but the Christian community, which, as it grew, inevitably began to take on a rough shape. A new word enters the Christian vocabulary, a word that expresses their meeting, their assembly, their community, the word *ecclesia*, which we choose to translate as 'church'.

Our principal source for what that rough shape was is the Acts of the Apostles. That charts the history of the community from its first gathering in Jerusalem as far as Paul preaching openly in Rome. It tells the story of how the shape changed and changed again to accommodate new ideas and new people. But, at the very beginning, immediately after the Pentecost experience, we are given two fairly detailed pictures of the principles and activities of the earliest churches:

'They met constantly to hear the apostles teach, and to share the common life, to break hard, and to pray. A sense of awe was everywhere, and many marvels and signs were brought about through the apostles. All whose faith had drawn them together held everything in common; they would sell their property and possessions and make a general distribution as the need of each required. With one mind, they kept up their daily attendance at the temple, and breaking bread in private houses, shared their meals with unaffected joy, as they praised God and enjoyed the favour of the whole people. And day by day the Lord added to their number those whom he was saving' (Acts 2.42–47). And later: 'The whole body of believers was united in heart and soul. Not a man of them claimed any of his possessions as his own, but everything was held in common, while the apostles bore witness with great power to the resurrection of the Lord Jesus. They were all held in high esteem; for they never had a needy person among them, because all who had property in land or houses sold it, brought the proceeds of the sale, and laid the money at the feet of the apostles; it was then distributed to any who stood in need' (4.32–35).

The passages need little commentary; they convey their own milieu to the twentieth-century mind. The emphasis is on teaching, on worship and prayer, on sharing meals. In this way, the love between them was deepened. And the other huge emphasis is on a communist attitude to property and possessions. It really does not need much more spelling out that they saw their shared life-style as communist rather than capitalist. It is a common myth in the capitalist West that the church gave up this communal life and common ownership because it did not work. There is no evidence to support that notion, and it is far more likely that as the churches grew more linked to the state after Constantine made Christianity the official religion, so more individual Christians lapsed, succumbed to the temptation of greed, and split off from the churches by buying property of their own. But there is little doubt as to what the policy of the churches was meant to be. Significantly, they managed to eliminate need and poverty among their own number by this means. They put the kingdom into practice, and showed the world outside how it could be achieved.

As churches multiplied, as they grew larger, as they included more and more people from different cultures, in particular, as under Paul's influence, they stretched into non-Jewish territory, so it became more important for Christians to build up a theology of the churches, a philosophy of what these increasingly varied groups were meant to be. As often, the writers of the New Testament sees things in pictorial terms. Paul, for example, describes the Christian community as being like a human body, each individual, each local group, being like a limb or an organ, quite different from its neighbour, and yet each one indispensable to the working of the whole. The analogy is spelt out in full in I Corinthians 12.12–26. Its climax for Paul is the understanding of unity, of one-ness about the functioning of the different parts of the body. It produces a mutual concern which meets the demands of love, and an example of unity which is itself a witness to the kingdom. 'God has combined the various parts of the body . . . so that there might be no sense of division in the body, but that all its organs might feel the same concern for one another. If one organ suffers, they all suffer together. If one flourishes, they all rejoice together' (12.25–26). And the whole body is Christ. It is this whole body that the world must see as Christ functioning in its own time. So that, as individuals and as local groups, you are a distinctive part of the whole; together, 'you are Christ's body' (12.27). In the letter to the Ephesians, the writer uses the same analogy in rather a different way: 'He (Christ) is the head, and on him the whole body depends. Bonded and knit together by every constituent joint, the whole frame grows through the due activity of each part, and builds itself up in love' (4.16).

Peter's analogy is a different one to make the same point. He sees the elements of the whole as being like bricks in a building, which will eventually become a temple for God, with Jesus as the corner-stone holding the whole thing up: 'our living stone – the stone rejected by men, but choice and precious in the sight of God. Come, and let yourselves be built, as living stones, into a spiritual temple' (I Peter 2.4–5). A Johannine analogy is the vine, with Jesus as the vine itself, and ourselves as the branches: 'I am the real vine, and my Father is the gardener . . . Dwell in me, as I in you. No branch can bear fruit by itself, but only if it remains united with the vine' (John 15.1ff.). And the New Testament draws other pictures. What it is important is that they are pictures and analogies – none are intended to be pushed further than they are stated. The church is described as *like* a body, *like* a building and so on, and some of the sillier claims for the authority of the churches have arisen from regarding these analogies as pseudo-scientific facts. The picture of the life of the churches, and the relation between them that we have is probably a great deal more loose-knit and free-wheeling than anything we would currently understand by the word 'church'. These early communities are measured and distinguished by the love that exists between their members, their dependence on love as they saw it in Jesus, and by the political system they organize for themselves to illustrate the kingdom, and thus to increase its effectiveness. What is *ecclesia* today will be measured, it seems to me, by the same things; the Christian community will not be confined, in other words, to a group that is called 'church'. It must be made clear, for example, that the church and the kingdom are not co-terminus; there is no biblical basis for identifying them with each other, though churches of the tradition are often tempted to behave as if there is. In the same way, the assembly, *ecclesia*, may itself be a more flexible shape than our modern concept of 'church'.

It may be so, because *ecclesia*, like so much of Christianity, has no specifically religious connotation. The first Christians came together in community, not as the result of a divine command, but because it was the logical expression of their love for one another, and the obvious means of demonstrating the kingdom culture. Like so much of Christianity, the gathering together into community is a natural activity, it is the result of what we already long for. Like love, like the kingdom, it is about enlarging not our piety but our humanity. We come together in order to become not more religious, but more human. Once we have glimpsed through the chinks of our ego defences, our inhibitions, that love is actually possible, and the kingdom of God is on, then we may begin to risk putting our arms around one another and discovering that to be in community, to be together, is the most natural thing in the world.

This natural, totally human way in which we seek community is in itself yet another signal of transcendence, another hint at what we might be when we are truly human. Hence the value that we put, say, on the life of our natural human family. I am sure that the mobility of people away from their roots, and the way in which the twentieth-century family unit has closed itself up with its two children in its brick box has severely damaged what the family is meant to be. Those situations where Granny is very much around, and where aunts and sisters and cousins are only down the road, are obviously far healthier. Though the family unit is stronger, it is therefore far less defensive, far less possessive, and far more willing to open its doors to the outsider. But even in that mutilated and truncated form which the family takes in our culture, there is still a sense of dependency and belonging which characterizes true community. Uncle Harry may live in Harrogate, or in New Zealand, but when the worst comes to the worst, it is to him that I am related, he is my flesh and blood, and he will look after me. That same seeking, that same human need, takes us into many different groupings and communities. It leads us to support and interest groups, where we meet others who share our passion for football, or pot plants, or model railways, or whatever. Many work situations have an element of community built in, and those that have not often try to create them. It is interesting that the caring professions in particular have increasingly felt the need to work together – group practices among doctors and dentists, teams of social workers, team ministries – and have found, too, that there are many things that can be achieved together which would not have happened through isolated individuals. The community is a natural human phenomenon because it meets a human need and because it makes human beings more effective.

Thus communities sometimes arise for those specific reasons. In the last decade or two, we have seen a massive growth of groups which exist in their own right, for the sake of simply being a group. A trip for example around the Festival of Mind and Body held annually in London illustrates their diversity. People are undeniably stretching towards a spirituality together, spirituality in the broadest sense. They are positively trying to become more human, more at peace, more loving. They will often, way outside the bounds of anything that might remotely be called religion, go through considerable pain or hurt, engage in strict discipline in order to reach some kind of fulfilment. Some have seeped into Western culture from the East, others have risen from our own insights, sociological and psychological. Christianity must learn not to regard such groups as in any sense second-rate or inadequate; here there are truths being learnt and love being practised which cannot but influence for good the society in which they happen. They will take the form of yoga, of breathing and relaxation classes, of encounter groups, of co-counselling, of dance. The growth of a need for a 'together' kind of spirituality is a very significant event in our time.

Just as there are groups seeking to learn love, so those whose concern is with the issues of the kingdom have found that they are clearly more effective together than in isolation. What I as an individual can do for the 'third' world is probably minimal, but allied with others, as a member of Oxfam, or War on Want, or Christian Aid, my effectiveness is multiplied a countless number of times. Thus those who want to effectively dismantle nuclear weapons will be part of the community which is the Campaign for Nuclear Disarmament; if you want to crush racial prejudice and violence with more than rhetoric, then obviously you are part of a community like the anti-apartheid organizations. So on into the other areas of caring – Shelter, Amnesty, the Samaritans and so on – all groups and communities who have discovered that if you want to be effective, if you want to exert pressure in such a way that policies and events will actually be changed, then it has to be done together.

Very often one emphasis feeds another. Those groups that meet to learn love for each other and to find self-fulfilment will also be effective in their witness and example. Those groups that come together to promote a cause find themselves loving one another in the process of being involved in a common task. And when those two areas meet, it strikes me that we are very close indeed to the true meaning of *ecclesia*. The togetherness of human beings needs to be of the right kind. It needs to be genuine community in that it really functions as a whole, goes for its ends, and supports and encourages all its members in the process. It needs to be a living example of what the world ought to be. But it also needs to be a grouping in which the individual is not swallowed up. It must make each human soul feel loved and free, just as we have defined it, indeed it must make each soul feel *more* loved and *more* free because he or she is part of something beyond himself or herself. The 'ecclesia' will be the place where the human being can say, 'Here I can be myself, here I belong, because these people are my people.' That balance is a delicate one, and rarely fulfilled, probably, but when it is, we have genuine family, true community.

Such community, to express it in terms of Christianity, is measured by the reality, the truth of its loving, whether it fulfils for those who belong the standards of love we discovered, of faith, repentance, spirituality, sensitivity, forgiveness and freedom; and measured, too, by its sheer effectiveness in changing its environment to be more like the kingdom of God, so that as a result of its existence, the society around it becomes more just, more peaceful, less fearful, its resources more equally shared. The truly genuine human community will be both love-truthful and kingdom-effective. If any human grouping is both, it is a true descendent of *ecclesia*, it is Christian community, it is 'church'. If it is neither, or does not seek to be both, then whatever name it gives itself, it is not.

In such a context, what we might call 'the churches of the tradition', the groupings that overtly take the name of Christ, find their right perspective. Some on the edges, serious deviations from Christianity, fall away. The majority of the mainstream churches may be seen as a crucial part of the whole movement. Part of it, but not the whole of it. The freedom of the Spirit is basic, and there never was any way in which God was going to be limited to human institutions. The churches of the tradition do then with pride bear the name of Jesus, but at the same time function as servants to the whole church and to the world, with humility allowing God to work anywhere and anyhow he wants. For that reason, part of the glory of the churches of the tradition will be their infinite adaptability. Just as the first Christian community changed many times even before it got to Rome, so the forms the churches have taken have been utterly countless. Jesus himself often seems the only common denominator between the forms. There seems no other relation between a frightened group gathered beneath the streets of Rome and the pagentry of mediaeval Catholicism, between a muttered gathering in a African clearing and a Sunday morning mattins in a smart English village, between a vast Evangelical rally in an American city and a tiny meeting for prayer in the early morning. The churches have taken a million different forms, and it must be part of the faith or the churches of the tradition that there are a million different forms yet to come. Nothing is sacrosanct, because in entering the world, God has made everything sacred. When the churches of the tradition have genuinely understood this, what they have done is, consciously or unconsciously, to reflect the culture in which they are set and look to the needs of those who belong at the time, while retaining a sense of the Christian tradition out of which they sprang. In other words, at their best, the churches have always been 'trendy'. There is something intrinsically right about the dignity of the Church of England, for example, in nineteenth-century England; about the colour and richness of the Catholic Mass in the glittering sun of the Mediterranean; about the stark simplicity of a wooden cross in a Lutheran church in Scandinavia; about the silence of a Quaker meeting in a university town sated with talk; about the free moving around and intoning for an agricultural population in Greece or Russia. The churches of the tradition are at their greatest when they humbly adapt to the culture and to the needs of people. They are at their worst when arrogantly clinging to dogma and liturgy against all the odds, when trying to impose one culture on another, and believing all the while that they are upholding some tradition in the face of advancing secularism. If the incarnation of God in Jesus is properly understood, then of course, God is advancing secularism, and a true clinging to the tradition is the cultivating of love-truth and kingdom-effectiveness in the here and now. Such things cannot be imposed from anywhere either from above, in terms of authority, or from behind, in terms of history. The true *ecclesia*, when seen in the churches of the tradition, will therefore be indigenous, in that it will grow from the culture in which it is set, and local, in that its prime task will be kingdom-effectiveness in its own context.

It is important to realize that the churches of the tradition, whatever claims they may make, are human groupings. The temptation to judge a local church as if it were a society for saints is enormous for those within it and those outside it. It is in reality a school for sinners. Its function in the local community is therefore a human one. It is called to demonstrate, within the limitation of human beings, what is true human community. In theory, a local firm with an industrial relations problem, a family that fears a breakdown of relationships, a school with signs of strain in the staff room, should be able to look at its local church community and say, 'Good heavens – here are fallible human beings, just like ourselves, with less in common than we have, people of different ages, types and classes, people who might in another context, not be in any sort of relationship at all, who are loving each other despite their differences.' That is the theory, and that is where it begins to matter that the loving is truthful. If it is phoney, if it is only a surface sociability, if it goes no deeper than the model railway club, then it does not fulfil its function. Once we are into love-truth, then the grouping becomes quite simply an example to others of how loving relationships and community can be made to work. It is a community within a community called to illustrate what community should be.

When the local grouping begins to function like that, or even to take that as its aim, then it also becomes to some degree kingdom-effective. It, too, like the kingdom itself, begins to act like leaven, it begins to affect the atmosphere of the firm, the family, the school. The town or village in which the church is set becomes a different sort of place because the church is there. Monica Furlong pointed out back in the sixties that, for all their failings, the churches were the only serious attempt at community and community living that most people could latch on to, that was easily available. For all their failings, churchgoers are at least attempting to function together, and are not cleaning their cars or cooking Sunday lunch in splendid isolation behind net curtains. For all its failings, the local church is seeking a role within community, it can mobilize talent, it can reconcile a variety of local interests. It can take on a overtly caring role – for the sick, the handicapped, the lonely, the elderly – doing what may be frankly regarded as ambulance work caused by an uncaring society. It can take on a prophetic role by raising the issues of the kingdom at the very points at which the rest of the community wishes to evade them. It can attempt such things for all its failings, and, since those failings will be more public than those of others, it will therefore take on the suffering involved. For the local church, the gap between what it preaches and what it practices will always be immense – it is a school for sinners – and everyone will see the gap. But by that vulnerability, the local church takes on the schizophrenia of the community around it, it absorbs the hypocrisy and failings of all men. In its caring, in its prophecy, and perhaps above all in its suffering, the local church takes on the task of continuing the work of Jesus himself. It aims to be Christ for its locale and its generation with all the risks and hurt that that involves. It therefore becomes a kind of representative community; it represents the kingdom and the command of God to love before the wider community in which it lives, and at the same time it represents before God, before the love at the centre of the universe, not only itself and its 'church' concerns, but the secular life around it. What the firm or the family or the school cannot pray for itself, the local church prays in its stead. It represents them. In short, the church as a whole takes over the role that in most religions is performed by the priestly caste. It is the local church community that enters the Holy of Holies on behalf of those around it, and returns to the secular community with the love and forgiveness it has received. Thus, along with pictures of the body, and the temple, and the vine, the New Testament also carries a picture of the Christian community as itself a priesthood: 'Become a holy priesthood to offer spiritual sacrifices acceptable to God' (I Peter 2.5). 'You are a chosen race, a royal priesthood, a dedicated nation, and a people claimed by God for his own, to proclaim the triumphs of him who has called you out of darkness into his marvellous light' (2.9). The whole church, the throng of *ecclesia*, of which the local churches of the tradition are a part, is a priesthood representing God to man, and man to God.

It is, of course, a derived priesthood, that is to say, there is only one real priest, one human being who really demolished the

God/man barrier, and that remains Jesus of Nazareth. The priest-hood of the community is only a valid picture in so far as the community does carry on his work. 'The priesthood which Jesus holds is perpetual, because he remains for ever . . . He has no need to offer sacrifices daily, as the high priests do, first for his own sins, and then for those of the people: for this he did once for all when he offered up himself' (Heb. 7.24–28). 'He has entered the sanc-tuary once and for all and secured an eternal deliverance' (9.12). So if a concept of the community that is love-truthful and king-dom-effective as a priesthood stands at the centre of Christianity as a religion, it is a priesthood derived from Jesus himself.

The priesthood of Jesus feeds the priesthood of the community, and, further down the scale, the priesthood of the community feeds those individuals whom the church calls its priests. How such a pattern emerged we are not really sure. It became clear fairly early in the Christian community that some sort of division of jobs was going to be necessary. 'The widows were being over-looked in the daily distribution. So the Twelve called the whole body of disciples together and said "It would be a grave mistake for us to neglect the word of God in order to wait at table . . . Look out seven men . . . from your number . . . and we will appoint them to deal with these matters" ' (Acts 6.1–4). By the end of the New Testament period, the variety of jobs does appear to have taken on some loosely organized forms; the table-waiters seem to have become 'deacons', generally responsible for the car-ing work, and there seem, too, to have emerged the key figures of episcopoi (overseers or bishops) and presbyters (or priests). Along with the other community tasks, these jobs have come down through the tradition in various forms. Most of the main-stream churches have them, although some do not use the names. To some of them, a historical chain, though frankly historically well-nigh impossible, is important; to others, it is the call of God to a job that matters. In all cases, the priesthood, the ministry, the job is derived from the priesthood, the ministry of the whole ecclesia, just as that of ecclesia is derived from Jesus. It must also be made clear that the priesthood of individuals is not only derived at two removes, as it were, but is also, as they say, 'only a job'.

That is to say, it carries no status whatsoever. The difference between priest and lay member of the community, between minister and people, between elders and the rest, is one of role, function and job, and not of status. Any such status would be quite unacceptable in the kingdom, and is therefore inconceivable in the church. Any authority held by people within the churches is strictly of the kind Jesus outlined for the kingdom, that is to say an authority based on service. Almost every problem that arises about orders and jobs within the churches is the result of misunderstanding on these two points. The priesthood of individuals is derived from the community and not imposed on it; and it is not a position held, but a task to perform.

But the New Testament does imply specific tasks passed down from the apostles to their successors within the community. Thus the priest is called to focus the blessing of God to man, he is called to express with authority the forgiveness of man by God, he is called to symbolically offer man's sacrifice of praise. Thus, albeit in a derived and much humbled form, some Christians are called to be themselves representative in a priestly sense, to be Christ, to take on the suffering of the community, to absorb its schizophrenia, to encourage its love, and to proclaim its vision of the kingdom. It is a task alongside other tasks of equal importance. Its edges are blurred, and it is right that they should be. But the commission is still there. From the moment when Peter realized who Jesus was, and gasped his realization of what the whole thing was about – 'You are the Messiah, the Son of the living God' (Matt. 15.16) – the responsibility of that knowledge fell on him. 'Jesus said: "You did not learn that from mortal man, it was revealed to you by my Heavenly Father ... On this rock, I will build my church ... I will give you the keys of the kingdom of Heaven: what you forbid on earth shall be forbidden in heaven"' (15.17–19). Similarly, when Jesus gives the Spirit in the Johannine account, he says to the disciples – 'If you forgive any man's sins, they stand forgiven' (John 20.23). A pattern is clearly established, and the successors of Peter and the disciples, whether in a historical or metaphorical sense, take on the same tasks. Jesus is the ultimate priest who has finally crashed the gap between humanity and its source. The *ecclesia* takes on the task of illustrating the result by its love-truth and its kingdom-effectiveness. The priest has the burden of being a focus on behalf of both the community and the world of what that implies for humanity.

The true Christian community, the real 'church', is identified by the quality of its service. 'We must be regarded as Christ's subordinates and as stewards of the secrets of God' (I Cor. 4.1). Its specific service is response to the belief that humanity and divinity have been reconciled; it therefore acts supremely as reconciler in the school, in the firm, in the family, or wherever people are set against one another. It is in this sense that, above all, it is called to represent its Lord: 'He (God) has reconciled us men to himself through Christ, and he has enlisted us in this service of reconciliation . . . he has entrusted us with the message of reconciliation. We come therefore as Christ's ambassadors' (II Cor. 5.18–20). The primary concern of the real church, then, is the world outside its own community; any concept of the church in this century needs to be judged in the light of Archbishop Temple's famous definition – 'The church is the only organization that exists solely for the benefit of those who are *not* its members.' If a church loses that priroty, it has lost its *raison d'être*.

All this, of course, is the theory of the thing. This is what the Christian community is meant to be. It needs little intelligence, and only a blink without rose-coloured spectacles to be aware that the churches, in their organized and institutional form, are failing in a fairly spectacular way. All the signs of the times indicate that there is no lack of interest in spiritual matters such as belief in God, the life and work of Jesus, the spiritual life, social concern. If anything, such interest is increasing. But, at the same time, there is a steady and increasing move away from religion in any organized, church sense. In simple numerical terms, people do not in general latch on to the churches of the tradition and see no particular reason for doing so. Even appearances at the folk-religion points of Christmas and Easter are now limited in Britain to a very small proportion of the population.

So, without entering a whole 'What's-wrong-with-the-church?' diatribe, let us look at the reasons for that. The truth is that the churches have effectively blocked up their own channels. There are certain very basic matters which have to be faced and put right before the churches of the tradition can again represent God as seen by Christians, and not until they do so will they be taken seriously by anyone else. First, they are now over-organized; they have built up a structure far beyond what is required to fulfil the task that they have been assigned. The structure has thus become important in its own right, and the churches spend most of their time, energy and resources on the life and the survival of the churches, time which should be spent on the world that God is trying to save. Second, they are now totally committed to the buildings in which the community meet, and once again vast amounts of talent and money are wasted on caring for and maintaining bricks and mortar. Such a priority is a scandal in a world starving to death and in a nation of increasingly indaequate housing. It also diminishes the Christian community itself. Christians are actually beginning to believe that they are responding to the love of God by putting up towers or renovating the heating. Third, and perhaps arising out of the first two, the churches in England, certainly, are too closely linked with the establishment, and I am not just referring to the so-called established church. Indeed, the Church of England does at least admit some responsibility for the needs of human beings within a specific geographical area. But in general, the churches in England still appear to be supporters of, if not the Conservative party itself, at least that middle-class respectable level of society that refuses to examine the reasons for the violence it is so ready to condemn. They give the impression of being about preserving the *status quo* against the movement of the Spirit and the building of the kingdom, they appear to condone the evils of racism and nuclear weapons and poverty by their deafening silence on the subjects. To criticize the churches as being right-wing is probably unjust as a general rule, but that is the impression they are giving, and until they consciously change their priorities, they will not be taken seriously by those they exist to serve, like the poor, those who suffer discrimination, those who are afraid. The churches not only have care, but must be seen to care and allied with others who are seen to to care. Their failure to do so has led to a fourth blockage – an over-enthusiasm to criticize and judge other human beings in direct contravention of the law of love, and a related unwillingness to accept people of other classes or creeds or colours or backgrounds. They will often make the right noises, but the fact remains that there are vast numbers of people who simply feel unwelcome in the churches of the tradition, because any welcome they are given is of a patronizing and superficial kind, and is dependent on them behaving as church members expect. Outsiders do not feel the freedom to be themselves, but a unspoken expectation to conform.

Fifth, and more evident, the churches entrusted with the ministry of reconciliation manage to continue to remain unreconciled. The firm, the school, the family in need of reconciliation will never turn to these churches, which so manifestly express hypocrisy. As long as individual denominations within the Christian community insist that the matters that divide them are more important than the task they have been given, then all effective witness, mission and service has seized up. Nobody is suggesting, or has ever suggested, that all local churches must look and feel identical to each other; each local church will respond to the culture and needs that gave it birth and shape. But, in the village where I live, for example, a village of a few thousand people, there are four denominations and five church buildings. They are all being maintained, heated, paid for. The churches are paying four different clergy to cover exactly the same area. Lay people are being recruited to do their jobs in parallel. We require, for example, four lots of Sunday School teachers. It is a nonsense. It is also dangerous nonsense, in that it sells a totally corrupt view of the churches, and it is sinful nonsense in that it commits the ultimate evil of an unwillingness to love and be loved.

Sixth, and last, when it comes to individual priesthood, it is, in most of the churches of the tradition, incapable of doing its job because it does not represent humanity. In the Roman Catholic church, it is able to represent only heterosexual, unmarried males;

in the Orthodox and Anglican churches, priests are allowed to marry, but they are still only representing a small section of their fellow human beings. Until the priesthood of the churches of the traditions includes both Christians who are female, and also Christians who are homosexual and allowed to say so, it is a priesthood so stunted that it cannot be effective, and virtually meaningless.

All these comments are not criticisms for their own sake. They are very serious matters, for all of them, in one way or another, illustrate that the churches of the tradition have, in some crucial areas, set themselves against any kind of accepting love. The lack of sensitivity and awareness with which they treat women, gays, outsiders, other churches, the poor and so on, the refusal to allow others freedom, the refusal to forgive, are very basic hindrances to their being what they claim to be. As a result of living with and having so few qualms about such blatant disobedience of the divine will, they are also totally ineffective in terms of building the kingdom. Make no mistake, it is of disobedience that we are talking. The will of Jesus on the unity of his people is quite clear. 'May they all be one . . . that the world may believe' (John 17. 20–21). The policy on discrimination for the early churches is also clear. 'There is no such thing as Jew and Greek, slave and freeman, male and female; you are all one person in Christ Jesus' (Gal. 3.28).

In the face of such wilful and often unrepentant disobedience, what are we to say of the churches of the tradition? First, I think, to re-iterate that they are part, but not the whole of, the 'ecclesia', the Christian community and tradition. If Christianity really depended solely on the churches of the tradition, we would be in a very bad way. Luckily enough, or rather, as part of the love of God, it does not. There is nothing sacrosanct about 'the church' in its present institutionalized and organized form, it has no divine right to existence or survival. As with Israel, it is always possible to let the vineyard out to others. There will always be what the Old Testament calls a 'remnant' who will be obedient if the majority will not. 'We are no better than pots of earthenware to contain the treasure' (II Cor. 4.7). Pots may be smashed, they are dispensable. It is the treasure that matters, and that may be stored by whoever is to be trusted. I think it was Harry Williams who expressed with startling clarity that it is possible that the churches could become the Anti-Christ, and that when they deny that it is possible, that is the point at which they *have* become the Anti-Christ. Those who refer to themselves as 'the Body of Christ' need to remember what happened to the body of Christ. It was mutilated and crucified and then resurrected in a quite new form. The real church, the true *ecclesia* has nothing to fear. It seems to me quite likely that, unless a mighty upheaval puts some of those basic things right, the churches of the tradition will not survive, simply in terms of numbers, for more than another couple of generations. Or if they do, they will have become so monumentally irrelevant to what is going on either in the world or in the real church that they will pass unnoticed. That does not, will not, matter very much.

What then, in passing, should be the relationship between the individual Christian and the organized churches? That, I think, will be a matter for the individuals. Some will be deeply immersed in their life and concerns, others will have rejected them totally and already be in the process of something new. Many of us will be hitting a whole variety of compromises in between. For the moment, I suspect it has to be a relationship of some kind, even of conscious rejection and constructive alternative. I fancy that a *laissez-faire* attitude of 'I don't need to go to church' is laziness rather than anything else. People who say that usually want to opt out of the hard bits of love and the kingdom as well. But the perspective that neither the kingdom of God nor the Christian community are limited to the sociological existence of 'the church' is very important. The churches as such may or may not die. They are certainly in many places at the present time at the limit of their useful effectiveness. Understandably, Christians whose prorities are the learning of love and the creation of the kingdom are beginning to look elsewhere for the Christian community, for the kind of 'together' experience that more accurately reflects the love of God, and is more convincingly committed to the ideals of the kingdom.

Where then are we to look? Where can the enquiring twentieth-century mind find evidence of Christianity and what it means if not in the churches? Where should it expect to see the new church being built, a church for the present and the future? Or to ask the same question in another way, where do we find Christian community that still retains the traditional faith, that still places people and love above religion and dogma, that clings to the values of Jesus and has not replaced them with man-made structures and prejudices? Any answer that we may give must of necessity be undogmatic, may well be little more than a guess. Christianity is not about foretelling the future. But I will nonetheless hazard a couple of such guesses, and suggest two strands, two phenomena, that such an enquiring mind might well note.

First, the growth of what used to be called the 'latent' church. It was a very fashionable idea, that, too, in the sixties – the idea that around, beyond the boundaries of the organized church was another church, its boundaries flexible, its membership unknown. From the theology that Jesus travelled incognito in every human heart, from the belief that he surfaced in every act of human love, there grew the concept of a wider community, perhaps not even aware of itself, perhaps not calling itself 'Christian' at all, but simply acting out the commands of God, finding love by what God has planted naturally in the human heart, working for the kingdom because love naturally led them to do so. It was a way of coping with the problem of the 'good pagan', it was a justification for absorbing what we chose to call 'men of goodwill' into the Christian scheme of things. Such a church was meeting unconsciously, and so un-selfconsciously, in all sorts of situations – work situations, meals, parties, pubs. It almost came to be thought that if God surfaced wherever there was love, so the church surfaced wherever there was loving community, as if Jesus had implied that if there were only two or three people together in his name, he could be there in the middle of them.

The idea is no longer fashionable. The need for identity and security has driven many Christians back to defining themselves as a separate caste, different from others, apart from the world, presumably superior, rather glad that they are not as other men are. Christians who are not prepared to risk entering the world in case they should be swamped by it, crucified. The strange thing is that, as the idea has lost its appeal, and the phrase 'latent church' has become a theological left over, the latent church has actually been growing by leaps and bounds. Those declining congregations, those dwindling numbers – where have they gone? Where are they now? What are they teaching their children? Did the vision of love that held them in the fellowship disappear? How dare we assume that because they lost patience with the organized churches that they abandoned the vision? More and more people have left the churches over the last two decades, and entered the world as their Lord did, risked oblivion, as their Lord did, and set about the task of revealing God where they are, by loving and being loved, by seeking first the kingdom of God and not putting it last. They have sought to become the Christ incognito. Others already there catch the love and the kingdom-vision, and may never have been taught to put the name of 'God' to their experience. But, as ever, it is not those who say 'Lord, Lord' who enter the kingdom, but those who do the will of the Father. 'Whoever does the will of my heavenly Father', said Jesus, 'is my brother, my sister, my mother' (Matt. 12.50) – they are the true family, the true community, the church. Like every human being, the church is tested by what it does, not by what it claims. Where the remnant are obedient, there is the church, there are the family of Jesus, the sons and daughters of God.

Thus, for the seeds that might well yet be seen incarnate as the church, we need to look again, and look deeply into God's created world. It was always true that the church that really mattered was the great community of lay people in work situations, homes, leisure situations, and now it is at those times and in those places that the church is erupting. Those work situations where people are working together effectively in teams and groups, the communities building up in schools, hospitals, community associations, clubs, pubs. Who knows what value we may ultimately come to put on some of those? We may return to the relaxation classes, the encounter groups, all the other places where people are discovering each other in a way that a cup of coffee after a morning service will never achieve. Thus, in a society in which human rights are subtly eroded almost daily, and what used to pass for democracy is threatened, it is inevitable that those who care about loving and being loved will find that they belong in political groupings – among other socialists or ecological groups – in causes, in charities, in the areas where the churches have showed real concern and vision, as in many aspects of industrial mission, in specialized areas like the Gay Christian Movement. Those who work for and those who support Oxfam and Shelter and Amnesty and CND and the rest are not just engaged in good works – they are the true church. We still may not be dogmatic. The boundaries are utterly flexible, 'we may not count her armies, we may not see her king ... but soul by soul and silently, her shining bounds increase'. The borders of the territory move in and out like a living, breathing organism. On such a church, the world looks and exclaims, 'My God, it's alive!'

Increasingly, too, and perhaps surprisingly, the latent church is finding it has a priesthood in its midst. What its specific tasks are may be uncertain, though its general purpose is the same as it always was. There are countless clergy, and the numbers are rapidly increasing, who have stepped outside conventional ministry. There are huge numbers of lay people who are present-ing themselves for ordination to the priesthood with no intention of ever taking on a conventional ministry. These are people who have trained theologically, accumulated pastoral experience, committed themselves to the worship of God on behalf of others, have received from the tradition the rights that are given to priests and then do not run churches, but return to the world, ask the churches for nothing. Some are used by local churches as assistant ministers obtained on the cheap, but that is not the real thrust of the movement. The churches of the tradition seek to pin them down with names like 'auxiliary pastoral ministers' and 'non-stipendiaries'. They miss the point. What is building up is a priesthood for the latent church. I work as an actor, I know of two other priests in that community. There are now priests who are teachers, social workers, health officers, nurses, publishers, policemen, stockbrokers, engineers, barristers, doctors, vets, supermarket managers. Some are active in their local churches, some have severed all contact with the organization, and put everything into the latent ministry. They offer to the latent church not leadership, not a way of organizing, but priesthood, a way for that church to be the church. Not surprisingly, it is in the world that God loved so much that he sent his Son, in the world where as a result people are beginning to look at one another with their eyes open, beginning to reach out for each other's hands, in the world where people are beginning to care about poverty and war and discrimination, where they are beginning to realize that the establishment in the form of governments and churches is offering no compassion, it is in the world where the needs are and where the love is that the true church is taking shape.

My second guess as to where a way forward for Christians together is showing itself is in 'community' in a more technical sense. At one level, the local church is an inadequate expression of Christianity, not through any fault of its own, but because its membership is necessarily part-time, spasmodic. Its individual members may be full-time in their devotion and in their attempts to serve and witness, but as a community, it comes and goes. There is not really the chance to learn love past friendship into hurt and pain and through to deep love and concern. There is not really the opportunity to grip a vision of the kingdom so hard that it has to be begun as a community. Thus many individual Christians, from both the organized churches and from the latent church, have often experimented in various permutations with living together all the time. The degree of sharing involved may vary considerably – it may be just the sharing of a house, it may involve the pooling of incomes and resources, it may seek to be self-supporting, it may centre around education or agriculture. It may involve the sharing of a whole life-style. There can be little doubt that such 'communes' are close to what the first Christian community was talking about. The level of relationship here may be more painful, but more truthful. The work for the kingdom may be more demanding, but more effective.

In many places, and, of course, in many generations, Christians have opted for a living together and a community experience at a much deeper level than society normally allows. It used to be a cliché to dismiss the religious orders as an evasion of real life. Any experience of a commune or of community life soon indicates that it is less of an evasion than many other choices we make. I cannot attempt to convey the breadth and depth of what is happening in the vast and varied experiences of community living. Only to maintain that, like the latent church, such experiences are growing, becoming more attractive to more people, beginning once again to find a trembling voice, beginning to carry their own validity, and to look and to feel like a church, like a future Christian community, like 'ecclesia'. Let me quickly sketch four communities, arbitarily chosen in that I know of them, and because they are very different from one another. There are thousands of others, and some who have no name.

I quote Harry Williams on Mirfield. 'Mirfield is in what used to be called the West Riding of Yorkshire, ten miles from Leeds on one side and five miles from Huddersfield on the other. It is a smallish town with its main shopping centre about a mile from the Community house.'[9] The house itself is called the House of the Resurrection, and it is a mansion which the community bought and extended. The community functions as a democracy, and it is financed by investments. Its Rule of Life begins, 'The Community of the Resurrection shall consist of celibate priests and laymen who combine together at the call of God to reproduce the life of the first Christians.' This is how the community goes on to describe its own task. 'The Community shall be occupied in pastoral, evangelistic, literary, educational and such other works as are compatible with its common life and worship, and are in accordance with the special gifts which God has given to its members, provided always that it be kept in view that the immediate worship and service of God must take first place in the lives of those who would truly after Christ's pattern minister to men.' Thus the community sets great store on the studying of the faith and the offering of prayer and worship. Many Christians who have been on retreats led by a Mirfield brother will have cause to know the depth of love and peace that such a community emphasis produces.

At the other end of the churchmanship spectrum, the emphasis of the community at Lee Abbey is on evangelism, of introducing people to the power and vitality of Christianity for the first time. This again is a large house, beyond Lynton in North Devon, across the Valley of the Rocks, overlooking Lee Bay. It is a stunningly beautiful setting. Here there is a community of lay people, sixty or seventy, many of them young, and some staying for terms as short as a few months. In that time, they experience community living. But this house has doors flung wide open, for all year round it offers holiday weeks, courses and conferences, youth camps and so on, with the community acting as hosts, together with a small team of chaplains. The gospel is preached in this atmosphere of community and relaxation that is engendered by the house, the site and the holiday activities, particularly long walks across the county. It describes itself as 'a centre for spiritual renewal in the church and society', and the community as 'responsible for an extensive teaching, training and evangelistic ministry at Lee Abbey and further afield'.

Both Mirfield and Lee Abbey, though vastly different in style, in commitment and in purpose, are part of the Church of England, and that denomination has gained incalculably from both communities and their offsprings. The most striking attempt to create a community that cut across denominational barriers is at Taizé. It is in mid-France, near the village of Cluny, near the town of Maçon in Burgundy. It attempts as a community all the vulnerability of Christianity – it is built in that the community may disband if this feels right. Brother Roger wrote: 'A small vulnerable community, held up by an irrational hope, the hope of creating harmony between the children of baptism and between men everywhere; a community of seventy men, Christians, called on to do a task which is quite beyond them, and, who in spite of their limited numbers, try to answer every appeal made to them, no matter from which direction.'[10] Unity is thus sought through service. Like Lee Abbey, its doors are open, this time for the meeting of human need, however it presents itself. Visitors to

Taizé will always be haunted by its worship, the ringing of the bells, and the simple plainsong offices that sound both timeless and utterly contemporary. It is worship with a starkness and a grandeur that seems to take it beyond religion into a kind of rhythm of human praise and distress. It is not an event in itself, but a place in which something might happen. That expectancy, that openness is the core of the community's being. The Rule by which it lives carries the same hesitant, pilgrim quality. 'If the rule were ever to be regarded as an end in itself and to dispense us from always seeking more and more to discover God's design, the love of Christ and the light of the Holy Spirit, we would be imposing on ourselves a useless burden.'[11] The journey is toward the unity of all people, of which the uniting of Christians is a stage. At the centre of the community is the huge Church of Reconciliation, and outside a notice which serves as both an invitation and a warning: 'You who enter here be reconciled, the father with his son, the husband with his wife, the believer with him who cannot believe, the Christian with his separated brother.'

Taizé has become a vast centre of ecumenical and international Christianity. At the other end of that spectrum, as it were, is a group of huts in a field near Bradwell in Essex, which is the original of the two centres of the Othona community. The second is a house at Burton Bradstock, in Dorset. The members do not actually live together, they are in a sense, a community of the heart. They may meet rarely, but they are committed to one another, and belong together. When they do meet, they are immediately living in community; for an odd week, or just a weekend, the individual is suddenly part of the whole, sharing its work, its study, its playing and its worship. That foursome is seen as the natural rhythm of the day, and any day at the community's homes will have elements of all of them, whether there are a hundred others there or just a handful. The worship is, un-like Taizé, Mirfield or Lee Abbey, completely unstructured. It cannot be otherwise. At Bradwell, it takes place in a stone shell called St Peter's chapel which overlooks the estuary, arguably one of the earliest sites for Christianity in this country. What happens inside is what any individual decides shall happen; the community risks its most important activity to the whim of an individual's freedom. That is symbolic of this community's core – that is why its members come and go, may be there, or may not be there – because it sees its community role as the place where the individual finds out who he or she really is. It aims, as it says of itself, 'to deepen the experience of Christian community and to study the relationship of faith and life with a view to more positive action in world affairs. It aims to provide recreation of a kind in which the whole personality is nourished in community.'

I mention these examples not by way of advertisement for Christian community, still less with any intention of comparing them with any other communities. What they have in common, and in common I am sure with a hundred others, is that by their natural settings, by their comparative isolation from the twentieth-century rat race, by the nature of their loving, and their mutual commitment to a common task, they have each developed in their own way something that feels almost natural, primal. There is a totally natural rhythm about rising early to deal with jobs on the farm at Lee Abbey, there is something very basic about talking and making a relationship among the rocks on the beach. There is a creative exhilaration about planting trees at Othona which comes quite unexpectedly. One day at Bradwell a child brought to me a baby bird that she had found with a broken wing – she had carried it all the way from the village. In that second, all the concerns about ideas and career and pressure disappeared, and all that really mattered in the universe was a child and a bird. And that felt right and natural, and happened only because the child and I were in community.

The real problem with such communities may be that they become an accepted way of life for those who belong. They risk losing confidence, they risk not being fully aware of how important they are. What they are in fact doing, often in obscurity, is setting up real channels of love-truth and symbols of what the future kingdom might be like. They are practical signs of hope for the future of the 'ecclesia', and the number of young people who seem to relate to Christian community in this form may be seen as some evidence of this. In their hands, in their example, in the success of their efforts, may rest not only the future of the true church, but the peace of humanity.

The true church has always functioned best when it is a creative symbol, when it relates directly to the community it serves. The first Christian grouping was to fulfil the task of the first disciples. The old parish church was a relevant reality while it was also a social and educational centre for the village. What the true church will do is continually shift its focus so that it is in a position to relate to those whom it is trying to reach. That is why my guess is that in a frantically mobile society, dominated by the media, it will be a latent church that will do the job because it can be equally mobile, it can surface wherever it wishes, it does not have to sit and wait for people to return, it can infiltrate the world with love and meet the world at its real points of stress, and not only on a Sunday in a suit. And my guess, too, is that when the stress gets too much, when the moving around has to stop, that men and women will look to those communities, large and small, that seem, under God, to have begun to master different ways of living together. The latent church, allied with the communities, could offer a genuinely alternative way of running our lives, an alternative to the pattern of greed and competition that has corrupted us, a way based on love, peace and justice.

For what we are speaking of, as ever, is not what it means to be Christian, but ultimately of what it means to be human. The latent church can afford to be, is called to be, utterly human, immersed in the ways of the world. The communities are creating a more human way of relating to each other and to the larger group, Lee Abbey sees itself as seeking renewal 'in society' as well as the church, Taizé is concerned for reconciliation with 'him who cannot believe', Othona looks for the nourishment of 'the whole personality' and for 'more positive action in world affairs'. The survival of humanity, not just the church, depends not only on its ability to live, but to live together. The function of the true church is to demonstrate that living with one another is possible. Christians are called to demonstrate mutual love and a love for those outside that will make life liveable for all men and women. Conveying love is, of necessity, an activity practised together.

The organized churches may or may not die. If that does not matter, I venture to suggest that what does matter is that the tasks of the church are still performed. The world as a community without Christian community within it might well become a living hell, it will probably blow itself to bits. There is no evading the true church, not for the sake of the church, but for the sake of the world. That is not to say that we will be any surer of the end of the journey than anyone else. In the search for love and truth, which is the search for God, we are surrounded by darkness and we are reaching into unfathomable mysteries. What the true church will symbolise is that we are not alone as we go. Despite our fears, and our pain, we are holding hands, so that we may feel one another's support and hope and love.

SEVEN

The Word and Other Words

There are people who attempt to use Christian belief as an escape route from personal inadequacies and harsh reality. They see belief as an alternative to the cruelty and dissatisfaction of worldly life. In fact, all they are doing is refusing to face up to the truth about themselves and the world. In order to achieve that, they have to duck and dodge all the questions of literary criticism and logic, reason and philosophy, all the standards by which other beliefs are judged. In fact, Christian belief arises out of the experience of what it means to be human, and demands not a distancing from human life, but a deeper exploration of it.

Similarly, there are people who identify the Christian life-style with a safe middle-class respectability, whereas it is, if it is to follow the path of its founder, inherently risky. While smart suits and church attendance still in many places cover up the frightened souls within, Christianity demands their exposure in genuine relation to other people, a mutual acknowledgment of our inability to love. Christianity is not an alternative to love any more than it is to rational thought. It is rather a struggle towards both, which is why it is not an alternative to politics either, and will take particular political stances. Properly thought through, it is hard to place Christianity far from the radical left, and the 'peace movement' part of the spectrum. Membership of the Christian community is not a sign of good intentions or of individual status, but engagement in a common 'together' task of renewing a broken world with the love of its creator.

The truth is that what passes for Christianity is very often nothing more or less than a reversion to childhood. A vast majority of people stopped thinking and feeling the religious questions before they reached their teens, and so their impressions of what Christianity is about is based on childhood memories. You believe what you are told without question, you believe yourself to be loved with no more than a minimal obligation to love in return, you have no need to be involved with the messier elements of public life and order, you go to places like church because you are told to do so. The rebellion against Christianity is a rebellion against childhood. The problem is there are forms of Christianity which perpetuate such an image, whether by a naive evangelical revivalism or by dependence on a ritualistic mysticism, and they achieve no more than an escape route back to childhood for those they suck in, and the alienation of those who wish to remain adult and will not take the trip. Meanwhile God is, Jesus of Nazareth died and rose for a suffering world, the Holy Spirit is unleashed, the Christian life-style evolves, a pattern for the kingdom of God is formed, Christian community pervades secular life, meeting adult human beings through their real experience and their honest needs. The exploration of Christian faith, life and community is an exploration of what it means to be adult and human. The dreams of childhood have to be honestly assessed and put away.

The snag in such a view of Christianity is that it lets in a subtle temptation, and this is the point at which the sceptic asks where a Christian differs from a humanist or a good pagan. At one level, there is no difference, need not necessarily be one. The frantic search by some Christians for a distinctive opinion on every subject as if we were in competition with the rest of the human race is merely childish attention-seeking. On the other hand, at a philosophical level, the Christian can claim, I think, to believe that the human values he tries to promulgate are not just advantageous, but right and true in an ultimate sense. The temptation to which I referred is that of believing that we have evolved this thing for ourselves. 'Natural' theology may be natural, but it is still theology, it is still about God and his ultimate purposes. In Jesus, God has passed divine responsibility to us, humanity is re-defined as a potential recipient of the Spirit, God's love is to be seen and known in human relationship, his kingdom is as political as any other, Christian community is about human community – but God is still God. Radical theology risks closing off the channel of movement from God to us. In other words, we must still ultimately acknowledge the activity of God, and his ability to reveal himself to us. Christianity is not an escape route, but neither is it a philosophy that we have formulated for ourselves to make life liveable. It is the revelation of the God that we have sensed. And sooner or later, we have to find among our resources for love-truth and kingdom-effectiveness the way in which that God speaks, the ways in which his intentions and purposes are made known. Sooner or later, like Jesus, the Christian must be asked 'By what authority do you do these things?'

It is within this context that, in the Judeao-Christian tradition, the Old Testament prophets are so important. Their significance is less in what they actually say than in that they saw themselves as spokesmen for God, that they had particular revelations from the heart of the universe which they felt compelled to pass on. 'God has spoken: who will but prophesy?' (Amos 3.8). And they were 'prophets' not in the sense that they foretold the future but because they believed that what they said would happen simply because they said it. In other words, their words were *effective*, what they said could change future events. When they use the traditional formula 'Thus says the Lord', they are assuming that they had set a course of *action* in motion. The prophetic messages thus for them illustrated the fact of God's desire to communicate with men and women, and further, his call for their obedience to his declared will. But most important of all, the potential effectiveness of the statements of God reflect what the tradition felt about him – his righteousness, his integrity, the unity of word and action; that with God, unlike ourselves, there is no gap between preaching and practice, between what he says and what he does. That integrity, that wholeness, is akin to our own awareness of God. The words of God which we seek must smell of the same integrity, they must be translated into action by definition if we are to regard them as authentic. This is, of course, the same quality of God that is sensed in the first creation story in Genesis, it is the way in which creation happens. God speaks, utters his word, and it is brought into being. 'God said "Let there be light" and there was light.' The word of God is communicated, but it is also creative and effective.

Christians vary as to where and how they believe God's creative word is revealed. The traditional distinction is between Catholic and Protestant. In its simplest terms, the 'Catholic' parts of the church believe that the authoritative word of God is communicated through the community of the church itself, its 'accumulated wisdom and experience', as Shaw put it, and most especially through its ministry, its hierarchy, those whom God has put in powerful positions within it. In its extreme form, it puts final authority with the Bishop of Rome as the successor to St Peter. Though it is worth adding that it is a fallacy to say that he is regarded as infallible in any general sense. Catholics believe that he is capable of making infallible statements, but only when he chooses to do so by speaking *ex cathedra*. In fact, he has only done so twice in the church's history, once to affirm the assumption of the Blessed Virgin Mary and once to declare himself capable of infallibility! The point, though, is the belief that God's authority and will are passed on through the leaders of the Christian community.

The Protestant view, on the other hand, the dispute at the centre of the Reformation, is that human beings are inevitably fallible, and that they must all submit to the authority of the divinely inspired scriptures, the sacred literature, that collection of books that we call the Bible. The sixth article of the Church of England sums up that view. 'Holy Scripture containeth all things necessary to salvation; so that whatsoever is not read therein, nor may be proved thereby, is not to be required of any man, that it should be believed as an article of the Faith, or be thought requisite or necessary to salvation.' It is probably true to say that the Christian community arose out of the ideas and beliefs that were available in the Old Testament, the reported words of Jesus, the letters of Paul and so on. But, of course, it is also true that the Bible was selected by the Christian community – its leaders decided which writings should be considered sacred and which not – and frankly it is hard to see now, for example, how the second letter of Peter slipped in, and other more edifying contemporary Christian writings, like the *Didache*, a kind of instruction manual, and the first letter of Clement, managed to get left out. In other words, what we really have is a 'chicken and egg' problem. Which came first? The Bible was chosen by the church, yet the church rose out of the Bible. Surely then, neither can be regarded as the ultimate authority since they are mutually interdependent. The extreme Catholic and the extreme Protestant must both be wrong. The ultimate authority, the declared will of God must lie behind and beyond both attitudes. The word of God is something else, something which inspires both Bible and church, and to which both must finally submit.

And it only takes a moment's thought, a short step out of the Catholic prejudice of slavish obedience to the hierarchy and the Protestant prejudice of endless quotations from scripture, to see where it lies. 'When in former times, God spoke to our forefathers, he spoke in fragmentary and varied fashion through the prophets. But in this final age, he has spoken to us in the Son' (Heb. 1.1–2). If you wish to hear God speaking, if you wish to know what he wants, if you want to see God expressed, if you seek his authentic authority, the place to look is Jesus. He is the expression of God, he is what God wants, in his person he is the declared will of God. The message that the divine wishes to communicate to humankind is not a system of community or a collection of writings, but the *person* of Jesus. He is God's last word. Which is why the Bible itself refers to him as the 'Word' of God. It is he who is the descendent of the creating word of Genesis and the effective word of the prophets:

> When all things began, the Word already was. The Word dwelt with God, and what God was, the Word was. The Word, then, was with God at the beginning and through him all things came to be ... All that came to be was alive with his life, and that life was the light of men ... He was in the world: but the world, though it owed its being to him, did not recognize him ... So the Word became flesh: he came to dwell among

us, and we saw his glory, such glory as befits the Father's only Son, full of grace and truth (John 1.1–4).

Yes, of course the will of God is made known through the church, both the churches of the tradition, and the wider *ecclesia* of human community, but only in so far as they reflect the real word of God, which is Jesus. All their ministry and priesthood, all their utterances, whether from a local minister or the Bishop of Rome, are, as we have seen, derived from the true expression of God, which is Jesus. Adherence to the traditions and statements of 'the church' is not to be used as a substitute for or as an opting out of obedience to the commands and promptings of the true authority, which is Jesus. The spirit of Jesus, Word of God, may like the wind blow from wherever it wishes, and it will not be confined to man-made institutions and communities or to the opinions of their leaders. The Catholic temptation is to worship the institution and its spokesmen as idols as a way of avoiding the development of a real relationship with the voice of God, which is Jesus.

But the Protestant temptation is to make an exactly identical idol out of the Bible. It can similarly be used as a screen between myself and the voice of God, and to call the Bible itself 'the Word of God' is totally misleading. There is a fascinating piece of mistranslation in the Authorized Version: 'Search the scriptures: for in them ye think ye have eternal life, and they are they which testify of me . . .' (John 5.39). When I was young, a Bible study course was published entitled *Search the Scriptures*. In fact, the writer is speaking of the *misuse* of the Bible: 'You study the scriptures, supposing that in having them, you have eternal life: yet although their testimony points to me, you refuse to come to me for that life.' Jesus himself is the Word of God, and no substitute, Bible or church, will do. The Bible itself must be seen in that perspective, and a great deal of damage has been done to the cause of Christianity by people who, out of their own need for security, have pretended that the Bible is other than it is.

The Bible is not a magic book, with an aura of light around it.

It is incredible to think that there are churches that will eschew all the trappings of ceremonial – flowers, or a cross and so on – and yet will happily place an open Bible on a lectern in a prominent position. Like an idol. It is not a book that will give messages from God when opened at random. It was not compiled by a succession of morons who gave their brains over to words dictated from the sky. To say, as I have heard, that the writers put the words down, but that the author is God, is a nonsense. The handy guides issued by those who worship the Bible tell you that the Bible claims infallibility for itself, and they usually quote II Timothy 3.16 as evidence that the entire Bible is literally true and morally perfect in its advice. In fact, of course, even if the Bible did claim infallibility for itself, it would be no different from the Bishop of Rome doing the same. And in any case, it does not do so. The verse reads: 'Every inspired writing has its use for teaching the truth . . .', which is hardly equivalent to infallibility. Yet I once had somebody walk out of a sermon in which I suggested that the Old Testament was wrong in advocating the stoning of adulterers. To claim that the Bible cannot be wrong at that kind of level is idolatory of a vicious kind. Quite recently in a church I knew, I saw a line of Sunday School children stand in front of a congregation and read out parts of the Bible that had been selected for them: they included some gruesome parts of the Book of Revelation; the burning out of the mark of the beast, the second death and so on. It was a very irresponsible action, totally un-edifying for those who listened, and possibly corrupting for the children who read out such images without comment or explanation. But the occasion happened because somebody believed that if it was the Bible, it would somehow be 'all right'. Similarly, I have seen leaflets put out to students that candidly state that 'there is one infallible Book', and asking for prayers that theological students will 'be scholars of the Book above all others'. Such an attitude to the Bible is at best silly, and at worst extremely dangerous.

It matters not least because it gives those outside the faith a totally false impression of the Bible. You still hear people say that if the Bible asserts that the world was created in seven days, and if science has proved the process to have been much longer, then the Bible is wrong, and Christianity disproved. And such an attitude only prevails because foolish people are still peddling the Bible as a history book and/or a scientific textbook. It is neither of those things, nor was ever meant to be. The sooner that is made clear, the sooner the Word of God, which is Jesus, can be made known.

So what is the Bible? It is, as we have seen, a collection of writings which the Christian community at an early stage decided to adopt as its sacred book. It consists of sixty-six works, although some, like Isaiah for example, are probably themselves compiled of several books. They are written by a vastly differing series of people and communities, all in their own historical and political contexts, over a considerable period of time. There are thus very different attitudes expressed about God, humanity, love and so on, and it would be surprising if this were not so. The works are of many different types. They include legend, fable, poetry, prophecy, letters, speeches, prayers, history and so on, all to be judged by different literary and historical criteria. It is not the product of a single mind, it does not express a single consistent attitude on any subject, and nobody ever intended that it should do so. It can be subjected to any literary criticism without diminishing the vision it proclaims, a vision that accumulates through the writers, communities and centuries that it represents. It does not need protecting, and so as time goes by and research goes on, we find out more about what it is and how parts of it came about. So attitudes towards the Bible can and will change.

Take, for example, those first few books, the world in seven days and all that. At one time, the first five books were attributed to Moses, but at some stage, people realized that he was unlikely to have written an account of his own death, or that he would have used place names which only came into being centuries later! At another, it became clear there is not one story of creation, but two. One begins with the universe and ends up with man (Gen. 1.1–2.3), the other works the other way round (Gen. 2.4–25). And then we find that one story calls God 'God' or 'Elohim' and the other calls him 'the Lord God' or 'Jahweh'. And as we go on in Genesis, we find that the two strands continue, a 'God' story existing alongside a 'Lord' story, and it looks as if two books have been almost accidentally combined. As we read on, it looks as if one or two other strands come in. So at present, many scholars believe that these first five books are a compilation from four different sources, which, being scholars, they call J, E, D and P. Whether those letters represent individuals or communities or oral traditions we do not know. It is, of course, more complex than that, but it serves to illustrate the kind of things that we discover about the Bible. And if the Christian community is to retain its integrity, it must be honest about such truth, not just in academic circles, but in its presentation of the faith. No one is doing Christianity any service by ignoring the issues of literary criticism, or talking and preaching as if they did not exist. There are truths about the Bible that scholars bring to light as the years go by – truths about the dating of parts of it which may not be as it first appears, truths about authorship, about the political context out of which various books came, the meaning of some of the symbols, truths about how the Gospels were formed – and these truths apply throughout the Bible. It is pointless for people to form a rearguard action to pretend such truths are not so. It is only those whose faith is pathetically weak who will fear honest inquiry. Nor must we fear passing the truths on. It is no great hardship to speak of 'words that John's Gospel puts into the mouth of Jesus' if you are fairly certain that the words attributed to Jesus are not authentic, or to mention 'the writer of the letter to the Ephesians' if you do not believe it to be the work of Paul. Large parts of the Bible are myth and legend, and there is nothing to gain from pretending otherwise. We may certainly not create new myths about the writing of it which simply conflict with the truth.

Just as the Bible is not to be used as a history book or a scientific textbook, nor must it be used as a written code. The New Testament itself is consistently adamant that it should not be used as such. The Christian faith is incapable of being formulated in the shape of a written document, and the documents must not be used as a by-pass for a living relationship with Jesus the Word or as a man-made limitation to the activity of the Spirit. The new covenant, the new God/man axis, is 'expressed not in a written document, but in a spiritual bond: for the written law condemns to death, but the Spirit gives life' (II Cor. 3.6). It owes its authority 'not to a system of earth-bound rules, but to the power of a life that cannot be destroyed' (Heb. 7.16). The Bible is not an infallible guide book of ethics for all time. Stoning adulterers is not the correct thing to do because some Jewish people thought it was. You cannot justify capital punishment in the twentieth century by appealing to the law of 'an eye for an eye, a tooth for a tooth' from centuries before. The fact that Paul in his day thought that women should not speak in church or that homosexuals would go to hell does not oblige us to think so now. And many of the moral questions we face today will have no answer in the Bible; there is no guidance on nuclear weapons because they did not exist then. It has nothing to say about tobacco or cannabis, and it knows nothing of a sexual morality in which contraception is a factor. No, I am afraid the Bible cannot enable us to opt out of making our own moral decisions, at least not without distorting it out of all recognition.

So am I simply saying that the Bible is not true? Only the very naive would pose such a simple antithesis between truth and falsehood. It depends, of course, what you mean by truth. I still value and use the little analogy that Bishop John Robinson drew from the modern strip-cartoon, like Andy Capp or Peanuts. You may reach the end of such a cartoon and think 'How true'. By which you do not mean that the story is a reflection of literal or historical truth, and that Andy and Flo, or Linus and Snoopy actually exist, but rather that it is true to life, consistent with human experience, revealing about the human conditions, enlightening, expanding one's view of the world, a valuable insight into daily living. It is in the same sense that the Bible is always very true.

And in that sense the Bible is to be respected and is placed by Christians in a supreme position among literature. To insist that there should be no idolatory of the Bible, no lying about its origins, no illusions as to its historical accuracy or moral authority, is not to lessen its importance. It is true that 'there is one mediator between God and man, Christ Jesus' (I Tim. 2.5) and that there is no other mediator in the shape of Bible or church, but it is also true that 'the sacred writings have power to make you wise and lead you to salvation through faith' (II Tim. 3.15). The library of books that we call the Bible is the source book of the Christian faith. It tells the truth about the nature of God and the nature of man and his world, and its writers were men of genius, inspired by the divine. It is a growing revelation of God's dealing with humankind and of our dealings with one another. Its stories carry the power of authority and conviction, its moral precepts ring true. And thus in my own seeking to describe and defend the Christian faith, I have naturally supported much of what I have maintained with direct quotation from the Bible. It is our sacred scripture, it is the source book of the faith. It posits the bedrock of dreams and visions by which we judge all else, and by which we live. In that respect, it is utterly authoritative and has been a consistent and continual inspiration to generations of the Christian community. It is thus one of the most precious resources that we have by which to achieve love-truth and kingdom-effectiveness. Alongside the Christian community itself, it is a mighty channel by which the Word of God, which is Jesus, is spoken to our race.

And so it is likely that Christians will be reading the Bible on a regular basis, so that its visions and priorities become part of them, second nature, felt on the pulse and in the blood. They will read it acknowledging its importance as a prime source document, and they will read it in a modern translation so that they will understand what it says. There may just be a case for the emotional force of a liturgy in seventeenth-century English; there is no case at all for reading the Bible or hearing it read in such language. If you wish to hear beautiful seventeenth-century words, read seventeenth-century poetry. But if you wish to hear God speaking through the Bible, then you must know what the writer is actually saying, understand his arguments, and you can only do that through a clear translation. The language of the Bible is not intended to comfort the faithful into a stupor such as

I have seen on the faces of many a congregation, but to convict and inspire and encourage. It is a continual provider of the Christian vision and the divine ideal. It will remain the safeguard against deviation and vague speculation, and it will be the inspiration to drive the Christian faith forward into new contexts, while placing the Christian firmly within the long and developing tradition that seeks to learn more and more about God's self-revelation.

There is a strange irony that those who make the most noise about the Bible are sometimes the last to hear what it actually says. There are Christians, for example, who wish to restore hanging or who approve of nuclear weapons who manage to ignore the simple biblical command 'You shall not kill' (Exod. 20.13). There are rich Christians in stockbroker belts for whom making money is a way of life, and who refuse to hear Jesus say 'Do not store up for yourselves treasure on earth' (Matt. 6.19). There is a difference between idolatory of the Bible which merely uses selected portions of it to bolster up one's own prejudices or justify one's own life-style, and an honest listening to it, a waiting upon it. I am suggesting that the grown-up Christian will take the Bible *more* seriously, expect more from it, than those who take it literally. When I studied theology in Europe, I was surprised to find a full course provided on 'the theology of preaching'. Preaching the Bible is very often in this country thought of as giving one's personal opinions or repeating the jargon loosely hung on a biblical text or passage. I am not suggesting that all preaching should be lengthy exposition, but we probably need to recover the awesome responsibility of what it means to be trusted with interpreting the sacred books, and we should learn to expect more from them when we hear them read or interpreted. Many of us who are called upon to preach will know the times when we have found ourselves saying things that we never intended because we felt compelled to do so. The Bible must be taken seriously, without fantasy or illusion, it must be seen as an ageless collection of human endeavour, our attitude to it must be grounded in commonsense, we must be willing to exert criticism upon it, literary, historical or moral. But the taking seriously will also allow for the enormous power that the writings unleash, believing that, like the Word of God himself, they are capable of creative effectiveness. It will acknowledge the inspiration it gives to reader, preacher, listener, an inspiration which may be far beyond what we expect. In one of the stories of Jesus's resurrection, the interpretation of the scriptures was a factor by which the two disciples on the road to Emmaus recognized who Jesus was: 'Did we not feel our hearts on fire as he talked with us on the road and explained the scriptures to us?' (Luke 24.32). Christians probably need to argue much less about the literal truth of the Bible and justify much less some of the very doubtful moral conclusions of its times. They need to appeal much less to quotation out of context. And they need to be more humble before such a massive piece of human achievement, its depth of understanding of the human condition and of the sense of God. They need to submit at a much deeper level to the Bible's power of inspiration, to allow themselves to be set on fire, to let the thing work, and let God speak.

Nevertheless, we must remember that God is spirit and is not going to be limited to anything we choose to package him inside. Jesus is the spoken word of God, and can be heard wherever he chooses to be. He is heard through the community and those entrusted with responsibility within it – that is the Catholic vision. He is heard through the Bible and its interpretation – that is the Protestant vision. But he will not be limited to either or both. To attempt to do so is to turn Christianity into a secret society, a club, an enclave where the passwords have to be known. And so, perhaps most important of all, we have to learn that Jesus the word of God is often spoken far from church or Bible, that it can carry the same power and authority wherever it chooses, wherever it sets hearts on fire. He is capable of making his will known, of revealing the word, through the awesome splendour of creation, from the mighty natural world to frail humanity itself. He is capable of making his will clear through other Christian writers, from Origen and Thomas Aquinas to T. S. Eliot, C. S. Lewis or Harry Williams. The revelation is a continually growing one, and God can use whom he likes when he likes. He may use such writers to re-express the age-old truths in such a way that we understand them afresh, he may use them to enlighten wholly new situations, he may use them to provide completely new insights into our condition, to create whole new grounds for faith, new patterns of theology. Without diminishing one iota the power of the Bible itself, we must not undervalue the glory of Christian inspiration as it continues. Words of poetry, prophecy, visions of God are still being written and spoken, and must be heard. And once we have accepted the principle that God can do what he likes, and make himself known where he wishes, then perhaps we have to learn to re-assess the place of writings from other great human traditions. We may wish to plead a more complete vision for those of Christianity, but God is perfectly capable of making something plain to us through the Koran, or the Buddhist scriptures, or the I Ching. These are not black magic, nor even pagan. They, too, with the other sacred writings of the world, stand within the human tradition of the search for God, for meaning, for wisdom and integrity. With what arrogance do we claim that the accumulated wisdom and experience of other cultures has nothing to say to us, that they are not and cannot be used by God? The business of the divine is the human – that is what incarnation is about – and, if that is true, then wherever human beings seek truth, light, love and peace, wherever they struggle to express them, then God is expressing himself, too. There are dangers in misusing the I Ching or Tarot, of course, as there are dangers in misusing the Bible. But as the global village becomes smaller, it will become more important than ever to see the Christian adventure as the human adventure, and to hear and recognize the word of God in cultures and traditions that seem alien to us.

In the same way, God is free to choose to express himself within that contemporary culture in ways that perhaps seem even more alien to us. Incarnation means that the whole of the secular has become sacred, and so we must not be afraid, indeed we must expect, to hear the will of God made plain through voices that call from the heart of contemporary society – philosophers, sociologists, commentators, writers who may not claim even a nominal link with the Christian community or Christian belief. Wherever the search for truth is honest, the voice of Christ is heard, simply because he is the truth. Recognized or unrecognized, openly seen or incognito, if it is true, it is God. If Jean-Paul Sartre opened up real truth about our lives, then the word of God was there. If Bertrand Russell challenged us to a more honest political morality, then the word of God was there. Many Christians can spend a lifetime focussing their attention on one place to hear the jargon endlessly repeated, and yet miss the vibrant creative word of God setting hearts on fire around them, because their vision of God is too small, too limited to their own vision, because they arrogantly desire to keep God for themselves, and cannot believe that God's love is human love, and God's truth is human truth, and that he may speak and be heard a million light years away from their theology or patterns of devotion.

This is, of course, once again the stuff of the latent church. Thus the contemporary Christian, once he has grasped 'the breadth and length and height and depth of the love of Christ' (Eph. 3.18) will not be surprised to find the will of Christ being made known not only in the church and the Bible, but in voices from the East, on bookstalls both Christian and non-Christian. He will expect no less to hear it from a friend in conversation, or in a chance overheard remark, or from communities committed to ecology or peace or socialism. He will be stirred, challenged, inspired, set on fire by what such people say or do, whether or not they bear the name of Christ. There will be prophetic pressure groups inside the traditional churches – industrial mission, the missionary societies, Christian organizations for social, political and economic change. And there will be groups outside – Councils for civil liberties, anti-racist groups and all the rest. And in all the clamouring voices, where there is truth, God's word is spoken. It is what we used to call 'letting the world write the agenda'. We are being told all the time what the will of God is, as human needs and human aspirations are placed before us. There is nothing sadder or more unfaithful than an isolated Christianity which carries on its own business in its own buildings, creating its own concerns, while the world pleads for love, peace and justice. There are countless well-meaning religious people who assert in some form that Christ is the answer, but who have never listened to the question.

So if we wish to hear those human questions which drove God's love to the extent of incarnation and crucifixion, the questions which make clear what his will now is for us, then we have to learn to shut up and listen. We need to recover the gift of silence, so that the questions and answers can actually be heard. We need to hear with humility the voices of other cultures and of our own. We need to let them get into our emotions and our core. There will be vast areas where God communicates not through words at all, but through gut reaction, through compassion, through vision, through conviction. That is why the contemporary Christian in a society hell-bent on technological achievement and material growth will be committed to support of the arts. God has spoken profoundly, creatively, effectively to generation after generation through music, poetry, visual arts, dance. He shapes lives and priorities in our own day through our music, film and theatre. He has always used myth, legend, magic, folk-tale to communicate. That is where the story of a virgin birth, for example, finds its proper place. Set in the Christmas tradition of angels and a manger, of a tree and lights and gifts, and the music of carols, it is a powerful and magical picture of an ultimate truth. And it communicates not by rational argument or by words but by artistic power, at gut level. It is that kind of magic, that kind of wonder that all art-forms attempt to express, and reach us at a far deeper level than argument or technology ever can. The greatest music of the world, for example, says nothing in any articulate sense, but nevertheless pulls out of us things that we recognize, ideals that inspire us and lift us nearer to the sense of wonder that we dream of. The arts are the product of the whole creative part of humanity that will not be satisfied with easy questions or answers, that seeks to delve into our dreams, our motives, our fears, our hopes, and they are a vital part of what it means to be human. They are thus vital channels of the love of God, and so vital places to hear the word. In the short term, the arts may appear easily dispensable, but in the long term they are integral to the sanity and health of the human race. They will not always present truth in the easy, packaged and palatable form that we can pass on to others. Their truth, like that of the Bible, will be that of integrity, of truth to human experience. The truth they present may for the time being be the truth of ambiguity as opposed to an endorsement of our prejudices. But ambiguity, for the present, is the way life is. That is the truth, and if that is the truth, God is there. And the greatest art of all leaves the way of hope open. The shaft of light, the possibility of salvation. It sows in us the gut feeling that the ambiguous struggle is actually towards something. Boris Pasternak described his own Zhivago poems as being about 'the joy of love, the pain of parting, the hope of religious experience'. It is there that art-forms lead, it is for that reason that they exist, and it is also for that reason that Christians will be committed to their survival.

There are those, too, who have made their lives into an art-form. Mother Theresa of Calcutta has offered more inspiration to the world than all the politicians of her time, and she will be remembered long after they are forgotten. The importance of the women huddled and singing at Greenham Common outside the death factories goes far deeper than the human fear that allows the weapons to exist. The young people who came together to make a record which raised millions of pounds for Ethiopia have a voice far louder than the stink of death from the desert. These are the voices of compassion in a world of fear, cynicism and despair. These are the people who care and are prepared to say so. They are an inspiration to the world, and creatively change our vision and our priorities. Like an art-form, they proclaim hope. They are the word of God: 'In you, the evidence for the truth has found confirmation' (I Cor. 1.6). The real truth, the real word of God, will always be evidenced in people and events, in what they produce, what they say and what they do. In that pattern, the church and the Bible find their place, but they are only a part of the vast spectrum across which God chooses to make himself known.

In the end, all other voices will be drowned, and the word of God, which is compassion, peace and justice, will sing out alone.

God is man, and human beings will finally not tolerate any lack of humanity or total rejection of human need. This deeply affects what the Christian community will mean by such terms as 'witness', 'mission' or 'evangelism'. Christianity is undoubtedly a missionary faith – it believes that if the faith were universally accepted, the world would be a better place. It will rejoice to see others find such faith. But that process is not the cold, limited exercise that some churches of the tradition easily promulgate. We are not asking intellectual adherence to a set of dogma, or an emotional response to a moving description of the cross. We are not asking for membership of a closed society, an alternative world of Bible-quoting jamborees or the wafer-thin world of a darkened church at Mass. Mission is rather spreading the word by actively influencing other individuals and society itself. It is about getting into the real world, and living a life in which the truth of Christ may find confirmation. It is not about carrying God like an ark into the pagan world, but about revealing and demonstrating that God is already there, alive and active. It is about treating men and women as God, since they are what he has become. Once they have been treated as such, then they can acknowledge their own status as his sons and daughters, by which we mean co-heirs with Christ, heirs, that is, to the kingdom.

All these things, the presence of the true *ecclesia*, the precious biblical tradition, the breadth of religious culture, the enquiry of our own times, the excitement of the arts and the lives of the saints, all convey to us and to our world the sense of awe and wonder which lies at their heart. And it is that at which we wonder, which is the ultimate truth. I mentioned the honest ambiguity of truth in our daily living, but finally truth is eternal and ultimate. There is a final truth, a final word: in the Bible, the great 119th psalm is a hymn of praise to truth's ultimate rightness. Jesus the Word is 'the same yesterday, today and for ever' (Heb. 13.8). There is finally no ambiguity. Once the Word is fully spoken, God is displayed in his world, the revelation is complete, that is quite simply the truth, and there is an end of it. But that is the final analysis. In the meantime, our task is love-truth and kingdom-effectiveness. We have to live the life-style of uninhibited love that God implies and build the society of mutual caring that he wills. We do so with the resources he has made available to us, and we know our direction from the voices around us that express the word of God.

EIGHT

Glimpses of Eternity

The aim is to love, to love each other warmly and fully, because we have seen that love is at the centre of the universe, and that we will be most ourselves when we are in tune with that. We aim, too, to create a society based on the love-principle, so that it too may be in tune with its source. In the process, we make use of human community in all its varied forms, and of the voices down the ages and around us that act as guides toward the goal. For most of the time, the process is one of struggle. The path is littered with failures and disappointments, broken hearts and missed opportunities, with conflicting advice and outright hypocrisy. But we live on the evidence of our highest moments, and only the occasional sense of the absolute centrality and certainty of the love-ideal convinces us that the road is worth travelling at all. Just now and then, a sensation deep inside that we have felt what the end of the journey is like, and that the feeling I had for this person or that was not a cruel illusion, that the dream of a world without war or poverty is not a vicious piece of wishful thinking. Bound as we are by time and space, just now and then in the shambles of our communities and the confusion of the voices, a moment of sharp, utter clarity, a glimpse of eternity.

Let me return unashamedly to that most potent of the signals of transcendence, the moment of human love. Almost every human being knows what it feels like, what it does to the gut, to the appetite, to the heartbeat. But like all the deepest and greatest emotions that we experience, it defies expression. Until, that is, we find a language that can contain it, when the words 'I love you' carry more than the words actually say. And we then begin to use other means. We sing love songs. I do not joke, we do actually sing them, we let tunes and their words do the job for us. We begin to touch, to take hands. We learn to kiss each other, to explore each other's bodies, to have sex – and at each stage, we are expressing more and more of that feeling for someone else which is defying words. These actions, these things we do, are standing in for the ideas that are too intense, too deep to say.

But that is, of course, not all they are doing. For each one is also increasing, adding to the depth of feeling. The taking of the hand is not just an expression of what is there, it is also effective, it is intended to provoke and promote love, it creates what it seeks. Sex arises out of a certain kind of relationship, but it also enforces and creates a deeper kind of relationship. If you have experienced sex with someone, you have not simply expressed your feelings for him or her, you have actually *changed* the relationship, you have put it on a different level, and that is precisely why it must be approached responsibly. And in terms of human love, many of the deepest relationships are able and willing to express that in the commitment of marriage, the mutual decision to accept pair-bonding for life. That decision is similarly the result of what is already experienced, and the promotion to a new level of relationship. A marriage, like all those other expressions of human love, is both symbolic and effective.

And it is that combination of symbolism and effectiveness, in the areas too deep for words, that I understand Christians to mean by 'sacramental'. It is because marriage is such that it is a sacrament. But then so was the song, so was the kiss, so was the sex. Marriage is the highest of the sacraments of love because it is about lifelong commitment. It is, like the others, a marking, a recognition in time of something that is ultimately, and unspeakably, true. And in the marking and recognizing of it, we open up new truth-possibilities. The action of the kiss, the act of sex, the act of marriage arise out of a human need to express, to mark, feelings that would otherwise lie dormant deep inside us. And in the act of expressing, the feelings change and grow. What we have done is scale down and focus a great eternal truth to the point where we can handle it. But because the truth of, in this case, human love, is genuinely eternal, there is no way that our focussing, our sacrament, can contain it. It can express it, but it cannot limit it. Nevertheless, our marking of that truth in this effective way is a deliberate view of the end of the journey. It is a moment, a decision, set aside, to create for a split second a possibility of what eternity is about. It is a presenting to ourselves an image of the dream by which we wish to live.

I choose the truth of human love and the sacrament of marriage because they are both recognizable in almost every human community. But the same principle applies to many other truths and our conscious marking of them. We do it all the time. A large part of our lives consists of feelings, instinctive reactions, and we could not exist if we did not to some extent put down markers. Thus my friendship with someone and my feeling for that person will be symbolically conveyed by my sending a birthday card or a Christmas card. And the sending of such a symbol effectively re-inforces the friendship. We express gratitude by the saying or the writing of the words 'Thank you'. We express grief by marking the anniversary of someone's death, an effective symbol of our deep determination never to forget that person. We all have days that are important to us, sacraments of time, paralleled in parts of the *ecclesia* as 'holy' days.

Similarly, as human beings we seek sacraments of place. It is not, of course that some places are sacred and some not. The idea of incarnation makes nonsense of such a distinction. But the church building or the street where we fell in love are places that we have marked as representative of something that we feel or believe. It is a way of handling what is too big for us. So particular places become sacraments of place. We make use of the created world to give strength to our search. In truth, the moon and the stars are simply *there*; when the sun sets, it is simply obeying the law of nature; when the water laps against the cold rocks, it is not saying anything. What we do is equate, for example, the stillness of the night sky with a universal longing for peace, we identify the long red streaks from the setting sun as a symbol of beauty, we meditate on the wet rocks to remind us of the created order stretching back to where people and personality had never been dreamt of.

We use actions, even games, to bring ourselves into the sphere of what we can handle. It has often been remarked that a game like Monopoly brings the enormous human cravings for money and power into a safe and manageable form. I can here release all my natural desire to be a selfish capitalist without truly making others poorer. And many other games perform a similar function, ways of dealing with our competitiveness, aggression, violence so that even those parts of ourselves which we fear can be brought under some kind of control. At a more serious level, drama schools, for example, teach students to trust one another, touch one another and so on by means of games and exercises which act as symbols of trust or physical contact, and also effectively create the means of relating that are needed. The world is, in short, full of attempts to bring truths and understandings that we believe to be of ultimate significance into the realm where they can be genuinely understood.

The whole process of theology, of exploration of the divine is, of course, just another example of the same thing, neither more nor less. The terms which we have come to think of as 'religious' or 'theological' are in fact sacraments of the more mysterious realities that we sense but cannot express. Hence as an effective symbol of the massive collision of the ideas of man and God that we are aware has taken place, we have the man Jesus. He is the sacrament of God at his most loving and of man at his highest. Thus too *ecclesia* is a sacrament of what human society is like, at best and worst, and which is in its turn a sacrament of the kingdom of God. The 'Word' is a sacrament of ultimate truth. The priest is a sacrament of the world's schizophrenia, in that the great gap that we all sense between what we practise and what we preach, the hypocrisy of what we wish to be as opposed to what we are, can be unloaded on to that public figure.

And all the time scaling down realities to a manageable size, focussing ultimate truths to where they can be spoken. There is nothing mysterious in the symbols themselves any more than in the love song or the kiss. It is what we do with them, the use to which we put them, the reality we make them serve, which gives them their power and their effectiveness. We use them as windows through which to see, through which to reach out and feel the reality. And the more we explore, the more we find that we may use all manner of objects and times and events, of persons and places, if we are so minded. It makes sense, of course. Since the whole point of incarnation was that everything should become sacred, so everything becomes potentially sacramental, useable in which to glimpse eternity. Like 'establishment', 'sacrament' is not a place, but an attitude of mind. We must not allow the fact that the religious organizations have tried to hi-jack the concept of sacrament, and to narrow it down to their own specific rituals, to blind us to the useability of everything around us for whatever purpose we choose. One of the primary tasks of the Christian faith is to help people to choose a purpose that is in fact sacramental.

If everything is potentially sacramental, then, some would argue, there is no need for any specific sacraments. If the sacramental life is a way of perception, then we are doing that life a disservice by narrowing it down at all. There are some Christians who therefore eschew sacramental *rites* as such, like the Salvation Army and the Society of Friends, although it is interesting that in recent years, there are increasingly numbers in those denominations who make use of the more specific sacraments offered by other parts of the Christian family, as if the need to focus has re-asserted itself. For it is the focus and the clarity of vision that any sacrament seeks to provide. It is there for weak human beings for when the words run out, for when any more speaking would just be the expression of somebody's opinion, for when the number of sides to an argument have reduced it to a vague generalization, for when a truth is faced with the prospect of 'death by a thousand qualifications', for when my feelings, emotions and prejudices have got so tangled up with the argument that I doubt the objectivity of anything that I believe – those are the points at which the moon and the stars are there irrespective, at which this date simply *is* the anniversary of a birth or death and a card will be sent, at which a Christian community might simply be quiet and break bread and share wine. Irrespective. Beyond everything else, whatever individual feelings and opinions may be. And it is because of that 'beyond-ness' that we choose sacraments in all their forms as our manufactured glimpses of eternity.

Such are the contexts in which are to be understood those specific moments that have been designated 'sacraments' by Christian communities. They are sacraments among sacraments, they are useable events, but do not exclude the possibility of others. They arise out of the human need to express objectively things that are by their very nature not objective. Hence marriage is a valid sacrament of human love, and probably the highest because it tries to hold everything within it. Exactly the same principle applies to other so-called 'minor' sacraments. We are increasingly coming to realize, for example, that the process of healing is a much bigger one than a trip to the doctor and a prescription for a set of chemicals. Even within the traditional medical profession, the awareness is growing that parts of a person play on each other; that, at the simplest level, physical symptoms may appear from causes that are social or mental or spiritual. Hence the increased interest in 'alternative' medicine, especially those parts of it that are committed to the wholeness of a human being; that to deal with the whole person may of itself prevent disease and illness later. And it is no coincidence that the word 'wholeness', the end of the quest, is the same word that the religious have in their jargon as 'salvation'. There are a million ways to the 'health', the 'wholeness', the 'salvation' of an individual, but they are all to do with taking the whole person seriously. This is to some extent what I think faith-healing is about – calling out of the individual some of his own resources for healing. I do not wish to reduce faith-healing to that alone, because for others it has been one of the million ways to health, and perhaps the one that has been the most effective. But I still suspect that it is unlikely that faith-healing is white magic. It is miraculous in the sense that all the sacraments are miraculous in what they draw out of us, of what resources they lock us into. In other words, the healing by faith, the laying on of hands, either in the glamour of a healing service or in the quiet of a dying person's room, is a sacrament of all the healing processes and arts; the skill of the surgeon, the faith of the healer and the healed, the hope of alternative medicine, the healing properties of the good earth, the love of family and friends, the move to a better environment. We set up a physical contact which will express that search for total wholeness, and which will, when performed, create something on the way towards it which arises out of concern, of peace, of assurance, of the faith of others. It is a deliberate enactment of the end we seek, so that we shall catch a glimpse of it, and move nearer towards it.

Similarly if two people have hurt each other badly, there is always the possibility that resentment becomes entrenched and their paths may never cross again. But it might also be that one or other decides to risk an apology. It may involve heart-searching, and a climbing down on a great deal of pride to come to that point. And when the words come out – I'm sorry' – and the reply is given and meant – 'That's all right. I'm sorry, too' – when perhaps those two people are able to embrace, those words and actions are sacraments not only of their friendship, but of that process of broken and restored relationship which is forgiveness. What is commonly called the sacrament of penance is, of course, nothing of the kind. It is the sacrament of forgiveness, and it clarifies, on the one side, a moment such as I have described, and symbolizes, too, the restoration of the God/man relationship. I am not especially in the business of arguing for the Catholic tradition of the confessional, and there is no doubt that it has been grotesquely misused. But I am also slightly suspicious of a pattern of 'I'm sorry' and 'That's all right' gone through as an internal dialogue in one's own room. It feels too glib, too easy. The process of forgiveness is more costly than that, and I can see the point of having to prepare, to assess the events which I most regret, of having to present them to someone else. I have on occasions divided a group into two, asked one side to read a 'confession' and the other the 'absolution' – for half of them, in effect, to say 'I'm sorry' and the rest to say 'That's all right', simply to illustrate that the sacrament of forgiveness is something open and mutual. Only a perverted form of it suggests that a Christian is under some obligation to confess to a priest. All two Christians are doing is acknowledging their failings in front of each other. All that the priest is asked do, charged to do, is to communicate the fact that there is redemptive, forgiving and restoring love at the centre of the universe, to say, in short 'It's all right' and to help the other to believe that ultimately it is just that. And it is that moment of forgiveness that is sacramental of all the other forgivings, of the deep need that we have to be reconciled to one another and to feel ultimately forgiven and accepted by whatever lies at the heart of life.

So many of the actions, rituals and traditions that have grown up within Christian communities have only focussed and expanded human sensations and needs. Some of those, it has to be said, have been sterile and pernicious nonsense, like cleansing women after childbirth, or the cursing of sinners, and they tend to disappear with the culture that invents them. It is those of value that have endured. The symbol of ordination to ministry is a sacrament of the specialness of each individual and his or her vocation to a unique role in the world. The symbol of confirmation speaks, it is true, of the reception of the Spirit, but is, I suspect, used more as a sacrament of human commitment, and has settled in most traditions to take place at an age when young people wish to stand on their own feet, and declare on which side they stand. As with all the other sacraments, we mess them up, we renege on the promises, we behave as if we saw nothing of eternity, we deny that it ever happened. But we have glimpsed, whether we like it or not. To have loved and been loved, to have felt forgiveness, to have seen one's uniqueness, to have felt committed, to have known the peace of being whole if only for a second in these or in any of the nameless sacraments in life, whatever we do with them later, nevertheless changes us irrevocably. In some strange way, we can never again be satisfied with less. They set our values and standards higher than we could have reached any other way. The individual sacraments, consciously chosen as parts of experience, enable us more easily to sacramentalize our whole way of life, to sharpen our perception of everything else.

The two central sacraments, baptism and the eucharist, exist in the same way and for the same reasons. They stand in a central position in the Christian faith because they are recognized by almost all its branches and because, traditionally, they are events that we were told to perform by Jesus himself. 'Go forth', he tells his followers, 'and make all nations my disciples. Baptize men everywhere in the name of the Father and the Son and the Holy Spirit, and teach them to observe all that I have commanded you' (Matt. 28.19). And in the Gospel accounts of the supper on the night before his death, Jesus enacts his own sacrament by declaring the bread he is breaking and the wine he is sharing to be effective symbols of his body and blood, which are to be effectively broken and shared the following day. In these accounts, the event is enacted and shared with the disciples. In Paul's account, possibly earlier than the Gospels, is the further suggestion that the event is to be consciously repeated in celebration of Jesus's memory.

'The tradition which I handed on to you came to me from the Lord himself: that the Lord Jesus, on the night of his arrest, took bread, and after giving thanks to God, broke it and said. "This is my body which is for you; do this as a memorial of me." In the same way, he took the cup after supper and said "This cup is the new covenant sealed by my blood. Whenever you drink it, do this as a memorial of me" ' (I Cor. 11.23–25). And Paul adds his own interpretation: 'Every time you eat this bread and drink the cup, you proclaim the death of the Lord until he comes' (11.26).

Similarly, after the Pentecost experience in the Acts version, Peter, when asked by the crowd 'What are we to do?' demands not only that they repent, but 'Be baptized, every one of you, in the name of Jesus the Messiah, for the forgiveness of sins' (Acts 2.38). Within a few sentences, we find them sharing a common life and 'breaking bread' (2.42). These two contrived events, the act of baptism carried through from John's ministry, and the breaking of bread in memory of Jesus's death, are quickly and deeply built into the experience of the Christian community.

Their centrality is not simply a matter of where they came from; it also arises from the vast scope in which they claim to be effective. If marriage is, for example, a sacrament of love, and absolution is a sacrament of forgiveness, we can see clearly that to which they relate, and the areas of life in which they are expected to change things. But the 'major' sacraments of baptism and eucharist are different, in that they relate to the whole of history, to whole personalities, to whole communities in all their aspects. If not instituted by the New Testament, they are certainly assumed by the New Testament at every point, because they are all-inclusive. It would be more convenient for a sensible, grown-up understanding of Christianity to dispense with them as archaic cultic rituals of their time. But they are built in at too deep a level, so that we have to come to terms with them. They are the sacraments of life itself.

Baptism is the sacrament of entry into life, and is thus unashamedly and rightly used as the initiation rite of the Christian religion. It has absolutely nothing to do, as clergy are endlessly telling people, with giving names to children, with preventing them from going to somewhere called hell, or with ensuring burial in consecrated ground. They are all myths and distortions that have arisen in cultures parallel to Christianity. Baptism is far more important than any of those things. It is about birth and re-birth. It is the Fourth Gospel that claims that 'you must be born again ... flesh can give birth only to flesh; it is spirit that gives birth to spirit ... no one can enter the kingdom of God without being born from water and spirit' (John 3.8, 6, 5). Baptism is the celebration of birth and re-birth in all its forms. The question of infant or adult baptism has ravaged the church for centuries. One of my first smiles at the pomposity of Christianity was when a fellow youth club member advertised a discussion group on the subject as 'one of the crucial issues of our time'. It is, of course, nothing of the kind, and the more I go on, the more I suspect it to be a gigantic red herring. Yes, of course there is huge significance in an adult who wishes to become a Christian from another religious culture or from the apathetic secularism of the West entering the community in the sacrament of baptism.

Its effectiveness as a symbol in such a context is very powerful indeed, not only for the individual concerned, but for the community in which it happens. But it becomes a total nonsense if the individual has been through it before, even as an infant. It ceases to be initiation at all, and loses its *raison d'être*. Millions of individuals and communities have also illustrated the power and effectiveness of parents presenting their children for the sacrament; for an event to symbolize and celebrate the arrival of new life into their families. There is only a problem if you are so small-minded as to reduce the sacrament of baptism to a mere declaration of consent to Christian belief. Of course an infant cannot do that. But that is only a fraction of what any sacrament is about. Birth and re-birth happens to individuals, to nuclear family units, to communities, to cities, to worlds. They are experiences to be celebrated, nurtured, shared, taken on for one another. The baptism of an infant – or an adult – is not the giving of a membership card, it is not joining a political party or a secret society, it is about the entry into life itself as much as the specifically Christian community. It involves decision and commitment at a deep level, not simply by an individual, but also by those in that person's immediate environment. Baptism as mere social custom, because Granny wishes it, is clearly not possible. But as a true sacrament, it is not finally dependent on our faith or lack of it. It opens up resources that are beyond the immediate environment, it locks into more far-reaching power. It is, crudely, something that love does, that God does, as much as anything that we do. And thus for the baptized individual, it becomes a marker, an event, a point, conscious or unconscious, at which love broke through to the personality in spite of the personality. Thus Martin Luther, a Protestant if ever there was one, expresses perfectly the Catholic understanding when, feeling his own faith collapsing around him, he clings on to the one fact that he knows, an objective event of which he remembers nothing and on which he holds no opinions, and says, 'I am baptized. Thank God, I am baptized.'

Thus within the rites of baptism are placed the conditions, the terms that will lead to 'life in all its fullness' (John 10.10). They represent humanity's attempt to express what it truly wishes for an individual, whether a new-born child or a convert. There is a kind of truth for the mother who has her child 'done' because she 'wants the best' for her child. So along with the celebration of life which is the basis of the sacrament, we also perform dramatically what we seek of life itself.

We seek, for example, to belong. That is why it is, in fact, an initiation rite. It is about the individual soul who has travelled a long time in the darkness and loneliness of the womb or of ignorance coming to an oasis of community, of other people – the family, the local church, the local community, the human race – and finding arms outstretched and smiling faces. It is a child lost in the desert, blind or lame, finding another group of children who will accept him as he is. Baptism is a sacrament of human welcome, of belonging and acceptance.

It is also, as we saw in the Acts account, a sign of repentance, of *metanoia*, of a decision to change one's mind, to set out in a certain direction. This is the element where an act of faith is made either by the individual or by the community on the individual's behalf. It makes real and effective humanity's age-old plea to have a second chance, to start again. It embodies not only birth but the potential for re-birth, it celebrates not only life but the promise of new life. It accepts the individual as he is, but does not accept life as it is, positing life as it might be, and what the individual might thus become. The possibility of change is built in.

Hence the central physical element in the sacrament of baptism is water – natural, clear, running, changing water. This initiation rite is not conducted with secret symbols, specially designed tools understood only to the faithful. This is the sacrament of the freshness of washing your face in a running stream, its components come from the created world. Its theology is literally natural. In the Jewish tradition, of course, the passing of individuals or a community through water sets up its own memories; it inevitably symbolized the turning point in their history when it seemed to their ancestors that the waters of the Red Sea parted to allow the nation to escape the slavery in Egypt, an event which gave birth to the nation in its own right. And the Christian tradition has consciously paralleled it with the baptismal experience of escape into freedom, that the dark, cold, enslaving bits of life are left behind – 'the devil' if you need to give it a name – and the promised land opens up ahead. But the water carries, too, the more natural and obvious symbolism of cleansing, of washing off the muck and grime that soil existence. Many a guided meditation incorporates the fountain that we imagine playing upon us. Baptism offers the active symbol, the reality of water, to make effective what otherwise we only dream of. A condition of new life, or re-birth, of the second chance, feels as though it ought to be a cleansing, a washing, a purifying, a passing away of the rubbish into the drain. So the symbol is water.

Technically, that is all that is required of a baptism – water and the 'threefold name' of God, Jesus and the Spirit. Within the traditions, other symbols have crept in to expand the vision of the best that we want from life. The calling by name, for example, symbolizes the total uniqueness and individuality of each human being; the giving of white clothing symbolizes the new cleansed soul putting on Christ like a garment; the giving of a candle symbolizes the task of the baptized now to pass on the light and love they have received to a dark and unloving world.

Perhaps the most interesting and the most effective addition is the tradition of tracing the shape of a cross on the brow of the baptismal candidate. It releases the understanding that life also incorporates death. The cross is nothing short of a gallows; the image is macabre and borders on the bizarre, and fits ill with a purely social custom. What the community is doing is marking the baptized person down as a potential martyr. The founder of the faith into which he or she is being initiated went to the gallows for blasphemy. It is quite logical that a disciple will go the same way. The degree of commitment that is actually demanded of the community is that this person will die if necessary for the sake of love and all the values that come from it. The marking of the brow places back in the mind the cost of discipleship – a cost well understood by the early disciples baptizing on the night before Easter in the catacombs under Rome, equally well understood by Christians in other parts of the world today, and increasingly being understood by Christians in the West, as established authority swings further away from Christian values. Infants baptized in English churches today may well discover the true and gruesome cost of discipleship in their lifetime. Many of those who fight for love and peace, freedom and justice, have already smelt it. Today's unrespectable campaigner may well be to-morrow's martyr.

This, of course, was already part and parcel of the meaning of baptism: 'When we were baptized into union with Christ Jesus, we were baptized into his death. By baptism we were buried with him, and lay dead, in order that, as Christ was raised from the dead in the splendour of the Father, so also we might set our feet upon the new path of life' (Rom. 6.3–4). Water parts the way to freedom, and it cleanses. It is also water in which we drown. For a second, the panic and then the stillness of death, of our deaths. But we are brought up out of the water, cleansed and gasping for breath, reaching for new life. It was after all *his* death, the death of Jesus, into which we were baptized, and we have already seen how ineffective that death proved to be. So we are also baptized into his resurrection. Indeed, that is the true and accurate meaning of the re-birth and the new life that we seek – nothing less than the resurrection of ourselves. Which is why it is the promises of baptism that are repeated in the liturgy for Easter, the feast of resurrection. 'If we have become incorporate with him in a death like this, we shall also be one with him in a resurrection like his' (Rom. 6.5). In short, the whole of human life, as they say, is there – the birth, the entry into life, the hopes, the dreams, the glories and the agonies, the love and the cost, and finally the death and the reality of re-birth which is resurrection. Baptism is the sacrament of a pilgrim's progress, of the journey of a soul.

It would be neat if we could say that as baptism is the glimpse into eternity of what the individual might be, so the eucharist is the vision of what community might be. It is, to some extent, true, but neither life nor thus the sacraments of life are as simple as that. There is a corporate element in baptism – it is about belonging – and there is an individual element in the eucharist. It has sometimes been over-emphasized: the concept of 'making my communion' verges on a spiritual picnic for oneself at the expense of everyone else. But God is person, the value of persons is central to all that is Christian, and so there is in the eucharist something uniquely personal, something on offer to the individual. But that said, it is, like baptism, a sacrament of the *whole* of life, and is therefore much, much broader in its intention than the inspiring or comforting of any individual soul.

Let me first get the terminology out of the way. I use the word 'eucharist' not because it is necessarily the best word to use – it simply means 'thanksgiving' and refers strictly speaking to the long prayer that precedes the breaking of bread – but because it is the word that seems to have become acceptable to most branches of the Christian church, and so may be used with the least offence. It is, of course, absurd that a community committed to love should have allowed quibbling with words to have caused the problems it has, but that is a problem for the institutions and need not concern us here. There is nothing offensive in the words 'mass' or 'holy communion' or 'Lord's supper' – like 'eucharist' they simply emphasize one aspect of the whole vast spectrum of ideas that the action represents. And no one term that emphasizes one aspect should blind us to the existence of all the others. For the purpose of this discussion, 'eucharist' will do, and the reader will substitute another term that is more homely if necessary.

The great power of the eucharist as a performed action is that it really is about everything – it is about bread, wine, Jesus, love, community, death, belonging, comfort, politics, repentance, greed, sharing, suffering, blood, flesh – simply everything. It is in fact an organized celebration with others of life itself, it is a thanksgiving for being alive. Its effectiveness as a symbol, its sacramental nature, is that, in so celebrating, we will become more alive in the sense we wish to be. It is thus the sacrament of everything, it is an attempt to enact a drama that will give new life, new meaning and new vitality to the world we live in. It lifts into the context of eternity all the things of earth, symbolized in a stroke of genius by two of its elements, bread and wine. It appears from the New Testament and from some early Christian art that bread and fish were once used as an alternative, but the earthy grittiness of bread and the dreamy extravagance of wine seem the ideal summing-up of a created world. And both to some degree made and cultivated by people, the work of human hands. The simple and central action of the eucharist is that the bread and wine are shared among those present, and so the intention is not just a thanksgiving for the resources of a created world, but a sharing of them. It is a sacrament of what the world might be if concern overcame greed, if sharing overcame possessiveness. There is no room for a second world in the eucharist, let alone a third. Geoffrey Beaumont expressed it beautifully, almost naively, in a hymn:

> For the bread on the table, and the wine in the cup,
> We thank the Lord, and we offer it up.
> It's God's way of saying that he'd give the earth
> For the sake of all around.[12]

The eucharist dramatizes the absolute naturalness of sharing and the sacrificial giving to others that is at the heart of things. I remember somebody pointing out to me that the round disc of bread which the priest – the principal celebrant of the eucharist – usually raises heavenwards before the bread is broken is remarkably the same shape as the world. It is a whole world we are lifting up, before sharing the rich resources. That is why, too, people must bring their own resources to it; that is why guilts and mis-understandings need to be cleared away first. I have celebrated the eucharist informally when people have placed a variety of things on the table: good things that are important to them, and bad things that they wish to lose there. Here nothing goes under the carpet, it is all on the table. The eucharist is a celebrating of life, a sharing of life's resources, a bringing of the individual's resources into the community, and a receiving of what the community offers.

I venture to suggest that however 'religious' the eucharist has become, however much mystery and mystique have come to surround it, that it is the most natural of organized human activities, that people coming together to celebrate, share, offer and receive on a regular basis would enhance and re-vitalize any community context. The life of any human unit would be made saner and healthier if from time to time it returned dramatically to this basis of what it means to be alive and human. For as well as a massive, regular, dramatized statement about the creation, it is also something that works for people, something that makes them look at one another in a different way. In most places now, the eucharist is preceded by the giving of the peace. It feels modern to many churchgoers because it forces them to break the reserve that the English in particular have long built into their religion. In fact, it is a very ancient custom that has been revived. It demands that the participants face one another, talk to one another, touch one another, and, in doing so, acknowledge their common humanity even if they have never met before. They wish peace for one another, they are in relationship, they are community. And the action symbolizes how quickly and easily that might in fact be achieved. Show that to the politicians. So what we are also attempting in 'eucharist' is a re-vitalizing of relationships, an establishing of community and of 'fellowship' (which would be quite a useful word if it has not become coated with memories of religious tea parties). There is no pecking order at the eucharist; those clergymen who create one have personality problems of their own. The actions and movements of the ritual should represent what an integrated, inter-related community would be when freed from guilt and prejudice. That is what those who do not attend 'eucharist' should see and feel if they did – a joy in being alive, but also an enviable relating by people to one another. What should attract is not how much or what strange things these people are able to believe, but what is showing in their faces, and how deep their concern for one another has gone. If those things do not communicate, it is not true eucharist.

But such things cannot be contrived. Which is why individual intentions have to have a reality and truth to feed into the eucharistic drama. Individuals are there to re-state and re-inforce not only their joy in life and their relationship to others, but to re-find the deep peace that comes from being in relationship with love itself, with God. For what 'eucharist' claims is that in thus meeting one another, individuals are also brought face to face with the source of life and love, are forced into an encounter not only with one another, but as a result also with God, the ground of being itself. This is achieved by centering the dramatic action not around a general concept of creation or a well-intentioned philosophy of life, but upon the specific event of the death and resurrection of Jesus. It is thus a re-enactment of the crucifixion; the cross rears its ugly form in the middle of the community and God's identi-fication with suffering humanity is re-proclaimed. And re-proclaimed in an active sense. We are speaking of far, far more than a memorial service for a dead hero; rather we are seeking to re-create the encounter with love that will re-charge the pat-tern of daily life. There was, the old adage says, a cross in the heart of God long before there was a cross on Calvary. The cruci-fixion of Jesus was not a whole new facet of God, it was a blinding illustration of what had always been true. In that sense, the sacrifice of the Christ was happening at the beginning of time, and will go on happening until its conclusion. In every twinge of pain, in every cancer, in every child suffering from war or in-justice, the cross goes on. It is stretched across the world, and men and women are still dying upon it. The historical sacrifice of Christ is unrepeatable – it was, as the Book of Common Prayer put it, 'a full, perfect and sufficient sacrifice' – but it is also an eternal sacrifice. In re-enacting it, in 'eucharist', what humanity seeks to do is to reach out and touch that eternal truth; not merely re-dramatizing a historical event, but tapping its current strength and purpose. It is an attempt to glimpse eternity, and that sacri-ficial love at its centre that created the cross of Jesus and so might also unlock the mystery of human suffering now and release that part of us which is forgiving and redeeming. The bread is taken and blessed as a symbol of creation, it is shared out as a symbol of community. But in between it is broken as a symbol of creative suffering. And it is in that breaking that we recognize love. That recognition is noted very early in the Christian tradition. One of the very first stories of encounter with the risen Christ is in pre-cisely this context; two disciples meet a stranger and he joins them for a meal. 'At table, he took bread and said the bless-ing; he broke the bread and offered it to them. Then their eyes were opened and they recognized him' (Luke 24.30–31).

Thus by extension, and with dramatic and poetic licence, the bread breaking becomes a symbol of the broken body of Jesus, and the wine shared a symbol of his flowing blood. Hence the tradition of the meal before Jesus's death, and Jesus's words 'This is my body ... this is my blood ... do this.' It is strange that those who make most noise about the literal truth of the Bible are least able to take this poetic and dramatic image on board in any literal sense. Those who accuse others of 'de-mythologizing' in fact de-mythologize on this point like it was going out of fashion. The early Christian community had no such qualms. 'Unless you eat the flesh of the Son of Man and drink his blood, you can have no life in you ... my flesh is real food; my blood is real drink. Whoever eats my flesh and drinks my blood dwells continually in me and I in him' (John 6.53–56). There is no case for an insipid watering-down of a faith as full of fire and guts as this. It is a vicious and terrifying understanding of sacrificial love. In Peter Shaffer's *The Royal Hunt of the Sun*, the Inca chief meditates with horror on the Christian habit of worshipping God, and then eating him. But what eucharist represents is that degree of closeness between God and humanity, the ultimate in incarnation, to be part of each other's metabolism. So that love, God, becomes, as an ancient prayer put it, 'nearer than breathing, closer than hands and feet'.

The bread and the wine become in a sense the body and blood of Jesus. In precisely *what* sense is a question that has bitterly divided Christians for centuries, for the most part unnecessarily. In the true context of eucharist, of thanksgiving, the 'how' is fairly irrelevant. It is clearly not merely bread and wine, but then nothing is 'merely' anything, since incarnation has sanctified everything. On the other hand, this is not magic either, there is no fear of bread literally turning to human flesh, so that a friend of mine could claim that his vegetarianism prevented him from being a Christian. 'Hocus pocus' is an adulterated form of 'Hoc est corpus meus' – 'This is my body' – that grew up because the eucharist was being made to look like a conjuring trick. There is no magic moment or verbal spell, it is the presence of the whole community and its willingness to perform and participate in the drama that gives it its strength and reality. It is the *whole* action of the eucharist, and the *whole* community performing it that validates it. It happens, this drama, on a regular basis in the middle of human community, not simply the articulate and gathered congregation, but performed on behalf of and for the benefit of all who live and work there. It is the cross set up on a hill near to all human life which may be responded to, or ignored, or acknowledged incognito. But it is there, bread breaking and wine pouring to represent the incessant flow of sacrificial human love. The human being who takes it on himself or herself to preach under the Word as a privilege is similarly cowed when presiding over this symbolic meal. The experience of responsibility for this, for handling the props of this drama, is difficult to express. It is both empowering and humbling, it seethes with both the confidence and the humiliation of being human. It is a privilege and a fearful task. But it also carries for the priest or president a unique sense of having touched the heart of things.

The Word inspires and calls us to achievements beyond our imagination; the sacraments, and the eucharist in particular, seem to release us from the struggle to achieve. Those who demand faith as some kind of intense experience that must be kept going, some permanent 'high', are missing half the joy of being Christian. Of course, a degree of belief is necessary for something like eucharist to have any meaning at all. But it may be no more than 'a grain of mustard seed' (Matt. 17.20), enough to get me out of my seat and to a communion rail. The rest may be left to love. In sacraments, God comes to us irrespective. Here more than anywhere, we need to learn to trust our instincts and experience.

Sacraments are not magic; nothing is conjured up. It is such silly attitudes that make Christian faith inaccessible to others. We manufacture glimpses of eternity, human constructions made at the times we need them out of the real things we have to hand – bread, wine, water, other people and so on. They are specific dramatic ways of saying that all these things are sacred. They are contrived illustrations of the Christian understanding of incarnation, the abdication by God of his own power, and the reality of

God at the human level. They are the flags and lights by which others may come to recognize that reality and they are to be used for that purpose, not as crutches for impossible beliefs. As the ordination charge of the Uniting Church of Australia puts it, they are 'those rituals and rites of meaning that in their poetry address humanity at the level where change operates'. They are moments of flashing clarity in a world confused, of the sacred in the secular, of the holy in the worldly. They are means to an end, and not ends in themselves.

The eternity we glimpse through them has to be real eternity. We have to sense within and through the sacraments, if they are the real thing, the end of the struggle. We have to sense the peace that might be at the end of it all, the unity that is drawing it all together. 'There are three things that last for ever; faith, hope and love' (I Cor. 13.13). Faith is where we start, and the 'greatest of them all is love'. The sacraments are there to reinforce our hope. And once reinforced, the hope must be seen to be functioning in daily life. As means to an end, the most important aspect of a sacrament is the leaving of it behind, the learning of its lessons, the exercise of its vision in a concrete world. The most important words of the eucharist were always in fact, 'Ite, missa est' – 'Go, mass is over' – 'Go in peace to love and serve . . .' There is no virtue, literally none at all, in having participated in anything sacramental. Those who think Christianity has anything at all to do with going to some particular place and going through some form of words or actions have missed the point entirely. They may need to do those things in order to *be* something else, but it is that being and living and loving that matter. 'Worship' is about spirit and truth (John 4.24); it is the valid and worthy response that we make to what we have sensed of love. Standing in rows, singing or listening to clichés is unlikely of itself to be such a response. Many of the churches of the tradition imply that 'worship' in the form of word or sacrament or both are their prime activity. Word and sacrament are the articulated dramatic expressions of Christian faith, and will probably need to exist to keep us articulate and to remind us of the great purposes of love. Some Christians regard those expressions as so important that they must be articulated as often as possible – weekly or even daily. Others regard them as so important that they will approach them as rarely as possible so that they are treasured and precious events that never become stale habit. But either way, no amount of knowing Protestant jargon or going through Catholic exercises will do as substitute for the real thing. The real thing is love, and we may need faith and hope, word and sacrament, in some form or other, to achieve it.

The eucharist and the other sacraments are originally and finally acts of drama. The theatre and religion have their roots in common. They operate at the level that poetry operates. Like all the arts, they arise out of a culture, and they feed visions and values back into it. They slip into the sub-conscious and change perspectives and priorities. As Peter Firth's eucharistic hymn puts it:

> We have felt the touch of love
> Within the bread this morning . . .
> And in the rooms and factories
> Where we're known by what we do
> We'll try to let this love of his show through . . .[13]

It is only when the loving lives of individuals and communities themselves become words and sacraments to others, to the world outside the specifically sacramental, that sacraments begin to make sense.

During the summer of 1985, I was working at the Festival Theatre at Pitlochry in the highlands of Scotland. Towards the end of the season, a member of the company, a talented young Scottish actress, was killed in a car crash on her way to a performance. It was incidentally interesting to see how, without my 'pushing' it, the fact that I was ordained become quite important at that moment to the rest of the company. We held a memorial service for Tricia in the theatre, in which her family and other friends in the business joined us. It consisted mainly of words and music which we knew she loved or would appreciate being spoken or played by her friends. After the service, we had coffee in the foyer, and some half an hour later, as we left, there was arched over the building a small, but complete and perfect rainbow. I *know* God does not work like that, and I cannot explain it, but it felt like Tricia smiling to say 'Thank you, I enjoyed that.' Strangely, hardly anyone mentioned it at the time, though I do not believe a single soul missed it. Our interpretations of the event may well have been very different, and yet common in that we used the rainbow to express a single hope that together we wished to articulate. The rainbow was natural, its timing either coincidental or miraculous. What we did was use it as a sacrament. The meeting of God's creation and our interpretation will to some extent have altered the way each one of us thought of love and of death. Those parts of the life of community that we call 'sacramental' are not mere religious exercises, they are articulations by the community for the wider community of what it means to be human.

NINE

At the End of the Day

The peace, the finality, the stillness of Tricia's rainbow feels like something very close to what humanity is trying to achieve. A point at which the struggle of living, not necessarily in extreme suffering, just the endless matching and mismatching of people and ideas, finally stops, when the things that happen to us have all happened and the world stops turning. Ultimately, the religious questions that humanity inevitably asks are about purpose and meaning, they are trying to see if any sense can really be made of the interweaving patterns of human relationships and aspirations. The final question is whether we are the victims of random chaos, or whether we are for some reason. The chaos theory remains for me denied by human experience at all levels, and so theology sets out to expand on the alternative. It is therefore obliged to hold ahead of human beings some hope. Once, when passing some forty-eight hours in Vienna, I spent much of the time looking for the ferris wheel. What with one thing and another, I never found it, and so never got to see it, and for months afterwards it became a symbol of missed opportunity, something beautiful and distant but never actually visible. Ironically enough, its silhouette is crystal clear on the skyline of a photograph I took – I could not have been far away, and even when I did see it, I did not notice it. Somewhere ahead, down a street we missed, is hope – a final peace and harmony and unity towards which we grope.

The movement, the dance of the Christian experience, is always a bringing of things together, of reconciling; the divine to the human, human experiences to each other, human beings to one another in love and in community, nations in peace. Things feel wrong when broken or fragmented and right when gathered together. It is almost as if Jesus exists as a magnet to attract everything to him: 'I shall draw all men to myself, when I am lifted up from the earth' (John 12.32). The progress to unity is sensed as the ultimately natural movement, the ending of divisions, the dismantling of barriers which have set up fears and hatreds and lack of trust. Unity is where love leads. The progress and the purpose are probably expressed nowhere better than in the letter to the Ephesians; it is the ferris wheel, the final vision, the ultimate reason for human existence and the most complete attempt to answer the religious question:

'In Christ, he (God) chose us before the world was founded, to be dedicated, to be without blemish in his sight, to be full of love; and he destined us ... to be accepted as his sons through Jesus Christ ... For in Christ our release is secured and our sins are forgiven through the shedding of his blood ... He has made known to us his hidden purpose ... to be put into effect when the time was ripe: namely, that the universe, all in heaven and on earth, might be brought into a unity in Christ' (Eph. 1.4–10). That is less glamorous than the more apocalyptic pictures, but it is still a vision of the end of time, when everything and everyone are united in him to become a perfect whole, a perfect unity, attracted to the centre by love which we saw as Jesus. And that will be us, and that will be the end, and that will be God, and everything can stop, and that will be peace. And the movement towards that final peace is unstoppable, because it is the natural movement of the universe, which is simply another way of saying that it is the original and ultimate purpose of a God of love. There is one thing that looks and smells as if it might stop the process, and that is death. The last Christian assertion is that, whatever it may look like, it cannot in fact do so. That is where the random chaos theory leads – to a rotting corpse of meat, pecked at by other creatures, to a belief that all human aspiration, all the values and virtues of the human beings we have loved, all the living and loving lead absolutely nowhere, that all acts of courage, selfgiving and love are ultimately meaningless, and can be snuffed out, rendered nothing at the random point at which the heart stops and breath ceases. Such a belief, such a faith demands a leap of the mind and imagination that I find impossible to make. It simply does not relate to the truth of human experience, it does not match the universe as it is. Death happens, it is in the movement, part of the rhythm, but it does not stop it. It is the progress that continues, because the call to unity and reconciliation by love is death-defying by definition, it is life-enhancing, life-affirming, life-creating. That is what the resurrection of Jesus *means*, whether historical event or not. As Sydney Carter's famous song has it:

> They buried my body, and they thought I'd gone
> But I am the dance, and I still go on.

Thus the commonest of religious questions – 'Is there life after death?' – is not in fact the ultimate religious question. It is understandably persistent; human beings will naturally look for ways out of dying, escape from the inevitable. Spiritualism and theories of re-incarnation are among the more sophisticated escape routes, and sub-Christian images of meeting beyond the Jordan are often frankly no better. The resurrection of Jesus does not by-pass human death in this way, it rather accepts it and then allows the movement to go on. The lesser theories – the 'everything-will-be-better-on-the-other-side' theories – open up the awful hypocrisies of insurance-policy religion which evades all responsibility for what happens now in the belief that all will be compensated for in some other world. It is sheer laziness, allowing all evil under the sun to run rampant. After the American bombing of Libya, I actually heard a sermon which admitted the horror of the event, but went on: 'But then I thought: what else can we expect in a world of darkness? ... The carnage of Tripoli shows us what happens when men and women do not surrender to Jesus.' It was a distortion of what Jesus is about, but more importantly a total evasion of all responsibility for the event or for any need to react to it beyond platitudes. 'Is there life after death?' is a sad, but valid question from confused humanity, but the more adult and responsible question is the joke from the walls of city streets: 'Is there life *before* death?' As to life, personal continuation, beyond death, one can afford, I submit, to being totally agnostic without dismantling an item of Christian belief. I do not know the answer, I have not encountered anyone who was ever dead. And it is not a question, frankly, that affects what the demands of love are in the here and now. Christians who spend time and energy speculating on the subject appear to have too much time on their hands. There is too much loving to be done, too much kingdom-building. The tasks for the Christian are evident all around us. And in making life more liveable for the living, in creating life before death, we are in fact participating in the very movement, the very process that will survive death.

We do not need to be afraid of the not knowing. The sense of God, what tradition has done to Jesus, the words, the sacraments, the building of the kingdom, above all the loving and being loved, these are all visions we sieze on, concepts with which we grapple, signs we follow. But we do so uncertainly, because we are not yet certain of realities we do not see. It is faith that gives us the burning inner conviction to cling to signs of transcendence and to see reality through them (Heb. 11.1). For 'now we see only puzzling reflections in a mirror . . . my knowledge now is partial' (I Cor. 13.12). Though we claim now to be 'God's children', 'what we shall be has not yet been disclosed' (I John 3.2). Still, out of the shifting patterns, humanity makes its attempts to visualize the end of the journey when 'we shall see him as he is' (I John 3.2), when 'we shall see face to face' (I Cor. 13.12). Although personal survival beyond death is not the core of Christian teaching, the 'when you die, you rot' theory does not honestly fit our experience. Research into what are called 'near death experiences', and particularly factors which such experiences appear to have in common, seems to indicate that something through and outside the experience of death is not unlikely. But to try to specify where or what seems to me an unnecessary and irrelevant exercise. Any such experience is bound to be at a quite different level, of a totally different order from anything we are conscious of now. There are no clues – there *need* be no clues – and guessing is futile. The only possible parallel is with the experience of birth. To try and describe experience beyond death is like trying to describe the physical world to a child in the womb, where it has no data, no experience of the same order to which to relate. From the fleshy warmth, a huge experience of birth, and then something so intrinsically different from what was previously known that there was no way it could have been described. If there is life, personal or corporate, beyond the grave, it is a difference of at least that order.

If, however, that picture from the letter to the Ephesians makes sense of our feelings and hopes of human experience, then it strikes me as likely that the unstoppable movement to the centre of love will not be stopped by death, that any movement beyond death will be in the same direction. In other words, what that passage implies, and I think the rest of the New Testament in various pictures supports, is that death unites us closer still with one another and with love, that we are in a sense drawn into the whole, so that finally we become one with another, part of one another, part of love, and so part of God. Such a theory appears to do nothing for those desperate for personal survival. It suggests the loss of individual identity into an amorphous mass, sucked up into love. But it may be that our sense of identity is itself earth-bound. It may be that the individual lost in the great family of love which is God will in fact find its true identity. It is speculation pure and simple. I just have a feeling that if I have to produce a theory of life after death, it will be along those lines. And the theory itself thus hints that the frantic question, 'But what is going to happen to *me*?', may be irrelevant, and ultimately selfish. In terms of love and the building of the kingdom, how important is my personal survival? Whatever form it takes, the Christian faith asserts that it will be in the natural order of things, and thus secure.

So the more important issue becomes not 'Is there life after death?' That is a question for those who prefer to dodge the more important issue, which is to do with attitudes towards death, how we approach it in ourselves and others, what we allow the fact of death to do to our lives. There is a story in John's Gospel which seems to make that distinction. Jesus visits friends and learns that one of them, Lazarus, has died (11.17–44). Lazarus's sister Martha puts to Jesus all those understandable, hurt questions that come from grief. 'If you'd come earlier, he wouldn't have died', and 'I will see him again, won't I, at (as she puts it) the resurrection on the last day?' And Jesus almost appears to say No, it's not like that. 'I' he says '*am* resurrection', implying that he is resurrection not at some unspecified future date, but *now*. And, as if to prove the point, the story has him bring Lazarus back to life, staggering out of the tomb, still bound by his grave-clothes, by the old attitudes to death. Jesus's last words in the story are to the family: 'Loose him: let him go.' The hurt questions, understandable as they are, are also finally fussy and irrelevant. What matters is the freedom released by an attitude to death that puts it in its proper place, that is, subservient to love and to life. It is love and life that Jesus exemplified and stood for, and his own resurrection, however you interpret it, is the startling demonstration of the victory of love and life over death. Death is not prevented, but what it does lose in the Christian priorities is its 'sting', its 'victory' (I Cor. 15.55).

What that means in practice about the Christian philosophy is that life and love are always stronger than death in all its forms. It means that the qualities displayed in their lifetimes by those we loved may be seized and lived out in the lives of those who follow them. It means that memories of love are impossible to erase by death. It means that no human being lives and dies without his or her life making some deep impact on the world. The world is changed deeply and irrevocably by each soul that inhabits it, for good or for ill. Our responsibility becomes therefore not to explain death, but to live life, to celebrate life. That will entail, among other things, helping others to a dignified and creative physical death, and preparing ourselves for that event, so that we may, in our own dying, be like Jesus life-giving. In *Tropic of Capricorn*, Henry Miller describes a time when he became aware of his own death, able to assess its impact on others, able to look into the coffin at his own inert and lifeless corpse. And in the act of imagining himself dead, he felt set free to live life more fully: 'Man walks forth from his open wound, from the grave which he had carried about with him so long.'[14] And the life that is born becomes more than existence. The ultimate questions of Why are we here? are not answered, but are met and challenged by a sheer *quality* of life, an ability to live life to the full, for its own sake, uncluttered by fear, death and guilt, the sort of life we know at our highest moments, the sort of life we respond to in others, the sort of life exemplified in the man Jesus. And it is the quality, not the quantity, as ever, that counts. What Christians call 'eternal life' is not about individual survival, longevity into eternity *ad nauseam*. It is a style of life, an attitude to it, and it is to be grasped not as a future possibility, but as a present experience. We are, if we bother to look, surrounded by eternal life.

It is that full quality of living that is the object of the human quest. In this century in particular it has been the grail searched for by poets and artists, writers and musicians, from Sartre to Eliot, from Picasso to the Beatles. There is a numbing feeling in our time that we are only 'partly living', that people are holding back, going through the motions, not risking anything and so missing out on the full value of being alive. We seek it for ourselves, and our responsibility is to seek it for others. There are points where people are held back from being properly alive by sheer obvious constraints, like hunger, inadequate housing, poverty, unemployment, bad health, bad education, discrimination on grounds of class or colour or gender or sexuality. To help others to attain eternal life, these things need to be attacked with all the force we can muster. This is what it means to fight death in all its forms. It is this richness of life, freedom in living that the Christian faith proclaims and strives for. 'I have come that men may have life, and may have it in all its fullness' (John 10.10).

And it is in that context that death – physical death – is to be assessed. Not the other way round. We do not live in the shadow of death, rather we die in the light of life. Death does not vanish, it cannot be cheated, but it has to take its proper and natural place in the scheme of things, and the scheme of things is about life and love, life-enhancing, life-bringing, death-defeating. Into that same context fall all the other speculative areas of religion that fascinate us so much. There is no reason to posit a geographical place called heaven, there is every reason to propose a quality of life that can never be diminished which we can begin to experience now. There is no reason to imagine devils and fires of hell, there is every reason to fear isolation from the centre of love, separation from life, the naked evils that stalk our world tempting us away from love to greed and selfishness and diminishing contact with our fellow beings. Sartre believed that 'hell is other people'. Heaven and hell are not rewards and punishments, they are the simple results, the consequences of our living. We have all been to both of them, we know what they taste like. And they are measured by the quality of our lives. We are in fact being continually judged. That other great bogeyman of childish Christianity, some future judgment, is in fact happening all the time. As long as life is there as a standard, other things are being judged. It too falls into the new context that Jesus is about. If there is such a thing as a final judgment, if such an event is necessary, it will not be about piety, but about results. Humanity will stand up to it when it has fully, riskily lived and loved.

But in terms of the movement which death cannot stop, I am not sure that the images of heaven, hell and judgment have any value at all if they imply a dividing up of creation. If the movement is unifying, if it is a drawing together, then there is no place for a philosophical system that divides people up into moral classes. The strand in the New Testament that passes judgment – sheep and goats and all that – seems to be more about how we live and judge and are judged in the here and now. The ultimate, but ultimate purpose of God, of love, appears far less divisive. The judgment is over – 'the Prince of this world stands condemned' (John 16.11) with all his capacity for death. By contrast, 'here is one point, my friends, which you must not lose sight of; with the Lord one day is like a thousand years and a thousand years like one day. It is not that the Lord is slow in fulfilling his promise, as some suppose, but that he is very patient, because it is not his will for any to be lost, but for all to come to repentance' (II Peter 3.8–9). In other words, far from the aim of the game being personal survival, coming out on the right side of judgment and making a personal entry to heaven, we are in fact all in this together. And of course we are! If the movement is drawing together all the scattered divided elements of the universe till we all find our home and our peace in the centre of love, then there can be none lost along the way. The movement will go on until everything and everyone is a part of it. The concepts of judgment, heaven and hell are worldly images on the way. The saving, the forgiving, the refusal to pass judgment on others, the willingness to give them life in its fullness, to allow them to live and let live – these standards lead not only to their salvation, their wholeness, their movement towards the whole, but also to ours. As Reinhold Niebuhr wrote, 'We are not saved until we are *all* saved.' The process of salvation is not the time-bound scheme that impatient human beings wish to impose, it is an eternal process which, until it is total, until we are dealing with a saved creation, will not be complete.

There are some Christians whose impatience demands an interpretation of some biblical pictures as a future historical return of Christ. Like all such speculation, it is a possible scenario, but by no means a necessary one. There are some Christians to whom this future return seems to be the only tenet of their faith. The real relevance of Christ's return is that it is even more like a thief in the night than such naive believers imagine. They are preparing for one thing, and missing another. Christ is indeed coming again. And again and again. In every piece of suffering, in every act of love, in every cry for help, wherever there is human need, there Christ comes. Like judgment, the Second Coming of Christ is a timeless, continual event which human beings, especially those who consider themselves religious, have a startling ability to miss. Do not misunderstand. It is not my intention to explain away those speculative future events which we call apocalyptic. The graphic illustrations of the Bible and other Christian art may indeed have varying degrees of truth about them: I stand ready to be surprised by what love can do. But for the sake of those who are put off the Christian faith by an apparent obsession at times with other worlds, post-death experiences and a speculative future, I want to swing the balance in favour of a faith that enables *this* life to be made liveable. I believe heaven, hell, judgment and the coming of Christ to be not fantasies, but realities, made real once the decision is made to live life to the full, to risk opening oneself in love, to enter the work of building the king-dom. Once we are engaged in those things, then the apocalyptic standards are credible, tangible and happening all the time.

Maybe it is Martha's question that persists a little. Will I see him again? How can I live such a life, enter that area of vulner-ability, if I have lost those I love, if there is no hope for the future? Can I face life in the event of death, even when I have put it in perspective? What happened to *them*? The movement is together, the movement is eternal, the movement is unstoppable. The whole thrust of Christian morality is to hasten and enhance the movement; it aims to break down barriers and bring people and things together. The divide between those who are alive and those who are dead is a seemingly implacable barrier. What we have to be brave enough to do is to search for unity there, too. The unity of love is also unity with them. That is what the Christ-ian tradition means by 'the communion of saints'. We are still in this together. Jesus is the archetype of a person we considered dead, yet whom we find walking beside us. He is joined, we are joined in the process by those to whom we have been tied by the bonds of love which we know death cannot undo. That is where the hope lies for them and for ourselves.

We are speaking of the end of the day, of final things, of ulti-mate purposes. It is the region in which all religions become speculative, and I would wish to assert my total agnosticism in all these areas. I will happily justify such agnosticism on the grounds that these are peripheral areas that have been used too often as distractions from the real business of the Christian experi-ence. What I am concerned to attempt is to guess, but to guess sensibly, out of human experience and not out of prejudice or wishful thinking. There is love, and that is, in one sense, all we need. There is faith to inspire love. But the third thing that lasts for ever is hope, and it is hope that enables love to stick. Fantasies apart, what are the hopes that can drive the modern Christian to keep faith and risk love? Behind the pictorial representations of the churches of the tradition, what are the final, but genuine ultimate truths which we Christians claim to hold out to our brothers and sisters? Once we have come to terms with death, with guilt, with fear, with meaninglessness, what hope is the universe holding out? What will be there at the end of the day? What, as they say, is the bottom line?

The fundamental Christian hopes grow inevitably out of the faith's ethical demands to love and to build the kingdom. It is thus that the hopes can be realistic. Out of the absolute centrality of love grows the assurance of the towering value of *person*. God is love and God is person. Jesus was person. It is as persons that we are accepted by, loved by and finally welcomed into the universe. There is nothing more valuable than the human soul. That affects not merely our moral behaviour but our underlying security, our basic hope. All risks can be taken in the sure knowledge that each human person is finally important. And that hope is not of itself dependent on piety or structures of belief. One of Paul Simon's simple love songs includes the words: 'I stand alone without beliefs – the only truth I know is you.' If there is one thing that psychoanalysis has revealed in our century, it is the rich treasures to be discovered on the journey into the self, the importance of valuing the self. That is not selfish or egocentric. A proper view of oneself, a pride in oneself, a peace with oneself is the springboard from which all true love and service begins. One of the things that the Christian faith in its grown-up form can do is value the person highly enough that love becomes possible. The true self is that part of us which is part of love and so part of God. It is, I suppose, what our predecessors used to call the soul. I therefore love the New English Bible translation of Jesus's famous call to discipleship: 'If anyone wishes to be a follower of mine, he must leave self behind; day after day he must take up his cross and come with me . . . What will a man gain by winning the whole world, at the cost of his true self?' (Luke 9.23, 25). The 'self' that is to be left behind is then presumably a false self, self-conscious, standing on ceremony, afraid to take risks. But the true self is to be preserved, because it is of ultimate value. Knowledge and understanding of that true self, confidence in it, makes it possible for someone to let himself or herself go – literally let the self, the false self go. As a child, I remember being told that as

Jesus died, he remembered my name, and knew that it was for me that he was dying. I would hesitate to use that emotional force on a child myself, but the image does describe the overpowering value of each human being in the purpose of creation. God's remarkable ability, as was Jesus's, as should be ours, is to allow each person to be himself or herself, so that they can let themselves go. And once each self knows his or her own value, knows in hope that his or her self is ultimately acceptable, then that person is free.

Out of the pattern of kingdom-building, there grows alongside that hope a second, which is that there will be a kingdom. That all the social activity in which we engage to break down barriers and reconcile people to one another, to other parts of the creation and to themselves are not just so much do-goodery, but are as we have seen an attempt to be part of and to hasten the progress towards unity which is already happening, not to change things for their own sake, but in order to be in tune with the way things are. Finally, goes the Christian hope, there will be a cleansed and redeemed creation, its barriers broken down, its guilt purged, its violence subdued, bought back by its creator at the cost of his own omnipotence. Whatever it may at times look like, the Christian values of love, peace, justice, freedom and joy are not just commendable objectives, they are the ultimate values. Those who preach them are often called unrealistic. The truth is rather that these are the ultimate realities, that when human beings have exhausted themselves with their greed and their ideologies and their petty power struggles, that these things will be the only things left, the only things that are in fact real. They are ultimately going to win, and any attempt to discredit them, any shunting of them to the sidelines, any refusals to take their demands seriously are doomed to failure, because such attempts place us already on the losing side. There is really no contest. The victory, as the New Testament continually reminds us, is already won. In one sense, the true *ecclesia* is a nation at war – fighting death in all its forms, including forms like apathy and self-seeking; but at its most vibrant, it is also parading the spoils of victory in its worship and in its witness. Those who do not work for peace, those to whom justice is a secondary matter, those for whom the freedom of others is worth only a minimal struggle, those who ignore the demands of love, who scorn compassion and caring, are fighting a lost cause, ultimately lost. I picked up a blessing many years ago from a fellow-priest, and I have used it many times since: 'God's love is going to win – may he work in all of us to that end.' The wolf is going to lie down with the lamb, and a small child is going to lead them (Isa. 11.6). Scenarios for the future based on any more aggressive ideology are simply wrong.

The Christian hope is that the future is utterly and ultimately secure. Maybe not the immediate future, maybe not for generations, but that ultimately each person is of ultimate value, and the kingdom is going to be ushered in. The future is not to be feared, not because of physical death, or self-inadequacy, or 'principalities and powers'; 'there is nothing in death or life, in the realm of spirits or superhuman powers, in the world as it is or the world as it shall be, in the forces of the universe, in heights or depths – nothing in all creation that can separate us from the love of God' (Rom. 8.38–39). Add to that the knowledge that the past is forgiven, that the universe accepts and loves us, both individually and corporately, as we are, whatever we have done. It was while we were 'sinners', not when we were good enough that Christ died for us (Rom. 5.8). Eternal life is the free gift of a loving God (Rom. 6.23). A secure future and a forgiven past makes, quite simply, a liveable present. We need not feel guilty about the past nor fear the future, and can therefore get on with living in the present. The now concerns, the now issues, the now relationships may safely become the ones that matter, without guilt or fear. Which is why the Christian faith is existential, created for each person by their own current decisions and priorities, and its morality by definition situational, shaped by each person and situation that we meet. The reason why so many books and sermons that try to present 'the Christian faith' as some great truth hovering somewhere away from the real world appear so bland, naive and childish, is because they are selling the thing in a vaccuum. And it does not exist in a vaccuum. There is no such thing as a Christianity which can be imported from the first century or from any other time, past or future, to be 'plonked' definitely on a different time and place. It is about living in the present, about relating to the here and now, both individuals and societies, or it is about nothing at all. Without a context, it is so much wasted breath. And what is on offer to the world in too many places is the smell of stale wasted breath.

The Christian faith is a historical faith. That does not mean that every legend in its mythology has to be regarded as historical fact. It means something far more important – that it exists for and relates at every point to the history in which it is set. Its Jewish background is that of a people whose belief was in a God who acted in history, in their battles and in their social and political life. Jesus was a man of history, in a real time and place, with real people of that time with real concerns of that time. To maintain a historical faith means that we do not allow it to get airborn, high-flown, inaccessible, but rather that we ensure its relevance to the historical context in which we live and move.

The Christian faith is also a traditional faith. That does not mean it has to repeat itself endlessly and meaninglessly from one generation to another. It means something far more important, that it must carry the demands of love and its vision of the king-dom and re-interpret them for every new context. The true traditionalists are those who will wrestle with the faith for each generation, so that the tradition does not die, but is preserved alive and relevant. I resent the hi-jacking of the use of tradition by those who simply wish to impose beliefs and ethics from some other time on to this. St Paul puts the distinction far better than I can: 'We are no better than pots of earthenware to contain the treasure' (II Cor. 4.7). The pots of earthenware can be smashed, re-moulded, made in some other shape, some other substance. The Christian faith has through history taken a million different forms, it takes across the world today a million different forms, some of which we may not even recognize. There are, I have little doubt, a million different forms yet to come. Our task is not to reproduce the forms. Our task is to preserve the treasure. And part of the task of preserving it is working out what forms are right for our times, how it is best contained and displayed for our contemporaries, with the simple objective that it shall make sense for them, that they will find it sensible, and so in their turn wish to preserve the treasure for generations to come. Those who present Christian faith as some historical theory or repetitious tradition that can be divorced from real relationships and societies are distorting it. Those who list a set of ethical imperatives that are to be imposed on humanity in all situations have completely missed the point. The faith is faith in the power of love, the ethic is to love – and love simply does not exist in a vaccuum, it is only, but *only* in persons, relationships, events and situations. To ignore them is to flout love. And to flout love puts you out of the tradition, on the losing side.

So, finally, what does it mean to be a Christian now in our time and place? I, too, would like to ask, What does it mean to be a Christian at all? But unfortunately there is no such question. Being a Christian *means* to be in a time and place. To say the Christian task is to say Mass or pray or read the Bible or convert others or all the other things to which we retreat is in fact to say nothing at all. For even those things mean different things to different people at different times in different places. We need rather to find how best to preserve the treasure of love in our time and place, to discover where love must challenge current trends and where it must wait in patience.

It is self-evident that the prevailing trend during the eighties has been, at least in the West, morally, socially and politically to the right. This is especially true in the United States, the United Kingdom and Western Europe. It was a trend that grew through the dissatisfaction of compromises in the seventies, and has clarified itself in this decade in a form of reactionary conservatism, based not simply on retaining our inheritance, preserving the *status quo*, but on positive conviction. As a result, it has succeeded in cutting across traditional class barriers, and given itself a base of popularity to secure its continuation and its ability to change the values and priorities of the society in which it grows. Its central conviction is economic, that market forces may be allowed to dictate how wealth is distributed without intervention by any outside interests, that good things will naturally rise to the top, and bad things fall away. Whatever the pros and cons of the economic argument – and it pre-supposes, I think, a highly optimistic view of what human beings will do with money – the theory results, as it is intended to do, in a competitive society, an 'enterprise culture', as the trendy phrase has it. The fear of losing is intended to drive us on to be winners. But, quite simply, not everyone can win. In other words, there will inevitably be in such a society both winners and losers and the social divisions that follow. In an extreme case like South Africa, we can see the divide along clear racial lines, but in parallel cultures, the same result is developing. There are those who temperamentally cannot keep up with a competitive rat-race, there are those who for various reasons – age, disability, being caught in the poverty trap – are just not able to join it, there are some of us who regard other things in life as more important than winning that particular race. And we and they become the losers, the lame ducks of the culture and we go to the wall. A recent newspaper cartoon showed a child pointing to a vagrant and saying to its mother, 'Look, Mummy, there's someone who didn't try hard enough.' The implication behind the 'market force' theory is that the harder you work, the more money you automatically receive. And that is just not true. In the rat-race culture, children are dying in an underfunded health service, the elderly are dying of hyperthermia, the unemployed are committing suicide, those who live in the inner cities are sending their children out to beg while the 'yuppies' build their smart houses next door, the disabled fight prejudice against them while their resources and services disappear. The losers go to the wall, and are told that they have only themselves to blame for being losers.

Money becomes the only yardstick. A person's worth in every every other department of life is judged by the amount of money at his or her disposal. In such a culture, money becomes a neurotic obsession. It is arguable that in recent years, the total priority given to cost-effectiveness and profit margins has been responsible for major disasters and loss of life on a cross-channel ferry, at an underground station and on an oilrig. When just before Christmas 1987, the greatest maritime disaster possibly of all time happened off the

Philippines, in which thousands of people perished in the water, it was reported in both major television news bulletins in Britain as the second item. And to what did it have to give pride of place? To the rumour of a take-over of one airline by another. That is the priority of a competitive society, and it is the value that it puts on human life.

A society that develops or allows an increasing number of losers is also potentially a dangerous one. To some extent, it therefore becomes important for those in power to suppress liberal or radical thought. We see that in its extreme form in totalitarian regimes, but the smell of it is around in less aggressive cultures; a gearing of education towards technology and business as opposed to disciplines that encourage individual thought; an increasing pressure on the media to support the rat-race, making sure that most of the press is owned by the winners; a willingness to censor if necessary; a deliberate reduction of the power of trade unions as the only place from which concerted action by the losers might spring; and calls specifically to the churches of the tradition to concentrate on personal morality rather than on social issues. Ironically enough, the level of personal morality among those in power is amazingly low. Events which would have been scandals a decade ago now appear easily forgettable provided those involved are among the winners. The real danger of such repression and its attendant hypocrisy is its potential for violence. The consignment of the poor, the elderly, the disabled, the hungry, the homeless, the jobless to the scrap heap is of itself a form of social violence, but it is worrying that the violence can become increasingly specific. The accumulation, accepted by society, of nuclear weapons is a willingness to tolerate the possibility of mass genecide to protect the culture, and is a tacit sanction for violence. The Rambo mentality arises not merely from the profits to be made from violent films (although that is part of it) but also from the explicit approval given to the principle of violent revenge by public figures like a United States president. Or by the British people being exhorted to 'rejoice' at the deaths of several hundred people in a sinking in the South Atlantic. It does not take a contorted logic to see that official approval given to violence on that scale will result in a lowering of the violence threshold, so that dubious violent decisions are then made by police and armed forces. A rationale exists for senseless violence in incidents like Hungerford, and the potential exists for riot in major connurbations. Violence breeds violence, and the movement is cyclical. The enterprise culture tends to regard the breakdown of law and order as a temporary distraction. In fact, it is part and parcel of the culture, an inevitable side-effect. The reason is moral rather than political or economic. The joke is that the proponents of the trendy new right refer scathingly to the generation ahead of them as 'the permissive' society. The whole point of the free market system is that it 'permits' forces to find their own levels. It therefore 'permits' and even applauds greed and selfishness, it 'permits' divisions to go on existing, it 'permits' hypocrisy and double standards in both private and public morality, it 'permits' violence. Indeed, it 'permits' all the worst elements of human nature to rise to the surface and succeed, it 'permits' all its opponents to suffer. In the eighties in the West we live in a society which is profoundly and comprehensively permissive. And sooner or later, people ask the question, If all these things are permitted, then what on earth is forbidden? It is a recipe for the losing of all moral sense and therefore for violence. And saddest of all in this context, it is a recipe for hopelessness.

It is not a challenge to which the churches of the tradition have risen with much fire. They have been fearful for their own influence, and reports like *Faith in the City* have been the exception rather than the rule. Even that report they have allowed to be adapted to fit the trend. They have still not taken a united moral stand on nuclear weapons. I would not have believed when I was ordained in 1968 that, twenty years on, separate denominations would still be weakening Christian influence, that women would still be barred from the priesthood of some churches, that gay men and women would be encouraged to lie about their sexuality or be hounded out. There is an amazing degree of tolerance within the churches to those who make spiteful attacks on anything vaguely liberal or which displays sensitivity, anything based on love and not on bigotry and prejudice. The churches are being

frightened into compromise with the trendy new right, providing
a field day for those who wish to drive the churches back to the
implacable stances of fundamentalism and cultic repetition.

Needless to say, the trendy new right runs directly counter to
anything in the Christian faith. If that faith has any public shape,
it will be that of a community where people care for one another.
To the trendy new right, such an appeal is 'wingeing'. So what is
the grown-up Christian to do? It is not simply a matter of politics.
It is a matter of retaining personal integrity, of taking up personal
responsibility in a society where less and less support, less and less
vindication, comes from the 'establishment' – secular or sacred.
In one sense, the politicians and the churches have both failed us.
There is little point where we are now in saying that the churches
ought to do this or that, or in campaigning for any particular
brand of politics. Being a Christian now will be less about belonging to one of the organized churches, and less still (despite the
building of the kingdom) about taking a particular political
stance. All will be tested by the way the Christian conducts himself
or herself within the culture. That will mean, I venture to suggest,
three things.

First, it will mean the Christian will not personally compromise,
but will maintain for the self at least the personal values upon
which the faith is based, the continual upholding in the face of all
temptation the absolute value of love, peace, freedom, justice; upholding it in both rational argument and in the way he or she
lives life. Second, we must ensure that the faith remains passionate,
that the gospel retains its fire and its guts, that it does not succumb
to the soft options of closed congregationalism, of television
hymn-singing or the retreat to bigotry. It must remain a missionary faith, and the values are to be spread with conviction. And
third, the Christian will seek out and co-operate with those who
share the values, if not necessarily the beliefs that gave them birth.
That is why the relationship with the arts is so central; the arts
are, like the Spirit, an enquiry into life that cannot be shut off.
The pictures, the music, the poems, the films of a generation can
instil values that no economic theories can erase. Christians will
be there. And co-operating probably, too, not so much in specific

political parties, but in the special interest groups – in the environ-
mental issues, in the peace movement, in social action charities, in
Third World concerns and many others.

In short, holding on until . . . And that is all right. Because
what the grown-up Christian knows is that, however dark the
days through which we pass, the values he or she holds are ultimately the only reality, indestructible, and finally bound to win.
That is why hope has to be as much a part of Christian doctrine as
faith and love. I am writing these words as the churches of the
tradition enter the week they call Holy Week, when Christians
not only remember but try to experience the week that led up to
Jesus's crucifixion, entering the dark, without support, without
protection, fighting silently like a nightmare against the forces of
evil as they gather. But the significant difference about Christian
darkness is that hope is built in, because we know it ends in
Easter, we know that the darkness cannot finally win. It is in that
kind of hope, that Christians will personally traverse the dark days,
knowing in the deepest sense that they are only 'days', however
many generations they may last. We will experience more and
more, I suspect, the sense of being pilgrims whose home is elsewhere, of wilderness wanderers heading for fulfilment in the land
that is promised. We live in what Joan Baez calls 'the meantime
years'. Around us in our time and society, people are increasingly
made to feel both hopeless and powerless. Men and women we
know will more and more be tempted either to despair or to settle
for far less than they ever meant to. More than ever, they will
need to be offered Christian hope, the message of resurrection,
that the past is over, the future secure, that life is here and now,
whatever the odds, that everything remains possible. There is
hope, the dream is not dead. There is a future, and we do, by our
priorities and our love, however long it takes, have a hand in
shaping it.

It was somewhere in the middle of life that you and I sensed
something to which I choose to give the name God. The value
of that sensation is vindicated in life at every point. The circle
will be complete, the pilgrimage over, the promised land reached,
when you and I become part of the whole, when love and the

kingdom are all there is, when the dream is shown to be utterly, utterly real. And you and I will be so much a part of it, so much a part of what I choose to call God, that when others sense it, we will be a part of what they sense. They in their turn will begin to traverse their own days which may be lighter or darker than ours, but they will be able to continue the movement because like us they sensed God. But what they sense will be a God that includes you and me, part of what they sense will be what you and I have dreamed and done. That is the hand we have in shaping the future. Who you and I are, what you and I dream and do is both what we sensed and also where we are going.

Resurrection. The universe finally rests. We end, as we began, with God. The grounds for the most ancient of Christian expressions: Alleluia.

A Kind of Credo

We believe that, whatever human beings may do to it, the creation is filled with love from its height to its depth.

That the man called Jesus showed us by his life, his death and the events which followed, that we are the object of that love, that we are accepted as we really are into the universe.

That in that confidence, we may risk following the spirit of love in our own nature wherever that may lead us.

That all morality is summed up in Jesus's command to love – to love ourselves, our brothers and sisters, and to love love itself – and that the command is to be worked out sensitively in each situation, creating a life-style based upon it.

That our brothers and sisters therefore have the right to love one another according to their true nature without prejudice, and the right to live in freedom from fear of sickness or hunger, ignorance, poverty or war, oppression or injustice, bigotry or discrimination on grounds of creed or colour, class or income, gender or sexuality.

Let those who choose to ignore the command to love understand that, whatever they may do, laugh or bully, seek to manipulate or render powerless, imprison, cause to disappear or kill in the streets or powerhouses, the true *ecclesia* will go on rejoicing in words of love, breaking bread and sharing wine, working in the cause of peace and singing the songs of freedom until all love's purposes are fulfilled, for ourselves, for our children, and for all creation.

NOTES

1. Peter L. Berger, *A Rumour of Angels*, Allen Lane 1970.
2. Henry Miller, *Sexus*, Calder & Boyars 1969; Panther 1970, p. 11.
3. T. S. Eliot, 'The Waste Land', Collected Poems 1909–62, Faber 1963, ll. 359–65.
4. Jean-Paul Sartre, *The Flies*, Hamish Hamilton 1946; Penguin 1962.
5. Michel Quoist, *Prayers of Life*, Gill & Macmillan 1963, pp. 91f.
6. Colin Morris, *Unyoung, Uncoloured, Unpoor*, Epworth Press 1969.
7. Eldridge Cleaver, *Soul on Ice*, Cape 1969, p. 91.
8. Anthony Wedgwood Benn, *Arguments for Democracy* ed Chris Mullin, Cape 1981, p. 130.
9. H. A. Williams, *Some Day I'll Find You*, Fount 1984, p. 311.
10. Roger Schutz, *Violent for Peace*, Darton Longman & Todd 1968, p. 49.
11. *Rule of Taizé*, p. 71.
12. Geoffrey Beaumont, in *20th Century Hymn Book Supplement* by members of the 20th Century Light Music Group, Weinberger 1965.
13. Peter Firth, in op. cit.
14. Henry Miller, *Tropic of Capricorn*, John Calder 1964; Panther 1966, p. 210.